Kinship

Kinship

An Introduction to
Basic Concepts

Robert Parkin

BLACKWELL
Publishers

The right of Robert Parkin to be identified as author of this work has been asserted in accordance with the Copyright, Designs and Patents Act 1988.

First published 1997

Blackwell Publishers Ltd
108 Cowley Road
Oxford OX4 1JF
UK

Blackwell Publishers Inc
350 Main Street
Malden, MA02148
USA

British Library Cataloguing in Publication Data

A CIP catalogue record for this book is available from the British Library.

Library of Congress Cataloging-in-Publication Data

Parkin, Robert.
    Kinship: an introduction to the basic concepts/Robert Parkin.
    224 p.
    Includes bibliographical references and indexes.
    ISBN 0-631-20358-3. – ISBN 0-631-20359-1 (pbk.)
    1. Kinship.
  GN487.P36 1997
  306.83 – dc21   96-45158
                                        CIP

Typeset in 10.5 on 12.5 pt Meridian
by Best-set Typesetter Ltd., Hong Kong
Printed in Great Britain by Hartnolls Limited, Bodmin, Cornwall

This book is printed on acid-free paper

Contents

Part II   Theories of Kinship

Figures

Preface

In the last ten to fifteen years, anthropology has undergone a definite shift away from traditional approaches to the study of kinship, formerly one of its central concerns. Initially, this was occasioned by statements that there is really no such thing as kinship, at least comparatively speaking, and that only by giving our attention almost exclusively to indigenous categories can anything worthwhile be said on the matter. Later, kinship came to be subsumed more and more under studies into gender, personhood, the body, ritual etc. – something reflecting this very same anti-formalist tendency. This tension between formalism and description – between modelling in the interests of cross-cultural comparison and the desire to give as exact an ethnographic account as possible – is nothing new in anthropology but is clearly intrinsic to it. Now, however, a feeling has arisen in some quarters that things have gone a little too far down the road towards this sort of deconstruction, and that to neglect kinship is to disregard a good deal of what any society explicitly recognizes.

This is not to say that the work of these last few years is to be rejected in its turn. Quite the contrary: there have been very real gains in ethnographic richness and specificity, in the sheer range and depth of what the subject now covers, in the inter-connectedness of previously demarcated spheres within it, and in our understanding of the relationships between thought and action, rules and behaviour. But this should not blind us to the fact that many societies still think in terms of lineages, affinal alliance systems, residence rules and marriage payments, while virtually all are still organized in families of some sort and use kin terms to

identify and classify relatives. Moreover, quite a number of anthropologists, refusing to be either seduced or browbeaten by the insistence of some of their colleagues that there is no such thing as
kinship, have persisted in developing traditional approaches, with
many fruitful results. Some recent conferences have indicated that
their twilight world is steadily becoming a new dawn.

There is thus a continuing need for a vocabulary to describe the
institutions, ideas and practices of the people we study with regard
to kinship. The fundamental aim of Part I of this book is to relaunch
discussion of this traditional, but far from exhausted, vocabulary,
doing so critically but sympathetically, and primarily, but not exclusively for the benefit of students. Using this vocabulary simply to
pigeonhole societies would certainly be to turn back the clock
unacceptably far. I hope to show, however, that used sensitively, it
is still more than adequate to cope with any descriptive task that
might be imposed upon it.

The idea of writing a book on kinship came to me while I was
teaching a course in Berlin in 1987 on the kinship of south and
south-east Asia. This was a time when the scepticism I have mentioned could be said to have reached its height (an indication, if any
were still needed, of my own position in this debate). It occurred to
me then that there was really no adequate introductory account of
the basic concepts used in discussions of kinship that was concise
and clear, did not mislead, and did not evade such wider issues as
the status of the anthropologist's concepts in respect of indigenous
ideas and practices, and the essentially social nature of kinship
everywhere. In making these my general aims, I have tried to
provide an account that is representative of conventional approaches to kinship rather than exhaustive of their entire history. I
have also avoided any attempt at explanations *per se* – partly
through a doubt that these are really possible in anthropology, or at
the very least premature – and have tried to be as unpolemical and
uncontroversial as possible in tone. Of course, no one can be
expected to write such a book in a totally neutral fashion, theoretically, and I certainly do not claim to have done so. My reply to
those readers who may disagree with some of what I say would be
that as much can be learned by reacting critically to a text as by
wholeheartedly agreeing with it.

Part I contains no references or ethnographic examples, in order to concentrate on concepts; chapter 15 (Part II) supplies these on a chapter-by-chapter basis. The remainder of Part II consists of four chapters, originally written as lectures but revised for publication here, which deal with various aspects of kinship theory in the work of those who have made themselves its main authorities. A number of issues dealt with in Part I therefore reappear in Part II in the context of the debates they have generated between individual anthropologists: this should provide a degree of revision. These chapters also contain conventional references and refer to ethnographic examples where these are relevant. The bibliography gives full details of all the sources referred to in the text, plus other useful works aimed specifically at students (marked with an asterisk).

I hope the book will be of value not only to new students but also to others wishing to consolidate or revise their existing knowledge of kinship. No single book can substitute for the hard work involved in getting to grips with exotic kinship systems or with what even the clearest and most perceptive anthropologists have to say about them. As with learning a foreign language, there are no short cuts to understanding kinship, a process which never really comes to an end. I hope that having been through the book once, the reader will find it useful to refer back to it continually in conjunction with other studies, both theoretical and ethnographic.

As already indicated, versions of both parts of the book have, at various times, been used in teaching. In addition, various drafts of Part I have been read through by a number of interested individuals, from fresh students to university teachers experienced especially in kinship. I am as grateful for their many suggestions as I am relieved that they felt able to leave so much of it intact. I have not always acted on their suggestions, however, and I suspect that none of them would really wish to be too closely identified with such a venture, even under the umbrella of my ultimate authorial responsibility (which I freely accept). I have therefore decided to leave them all in decent anonymity.

Robert Parkin
Oxford

Part I
Basic Concepts

1

Introductory

Kinship and Anthropology

All human societies have kinship, that is, they all impose some privileged cultural order over the biological universals of sexual relations and continuous human reproduction through birth. In many societies kinship even appears to be the sole or main structuring factor, and it is especially these societies that have traditionally interested anthropologists the most.

It is important to realize at the outset that, while the biologist studies kinship in the physical sense, for the social anthropologist kinship is not biology, but particular social or cultural interpretations of the biological universals just mentioned. The fact that the interpretation made by any one society is selective about the options theoretically open to it accounts for the considerable variety of kinship systems that humanity has created. The interpretation the reader of this book is most likely to be familiar with is the modern, Western, 'scientific' one, and he or she may feel that it is the only 'true' one. It is far from being the only one, however, even in Western societies themselves, and the question whether or not it is true or correct has little relevance for the anthropologist seeking to understand the interpretations of the world's other peoples.

This is not to deny the reality of the physical world, nor the validity of biological accounts in themselves. Given their history of mutual misunderstanding, it is worth reflecting a little further on the contrasts between the two approaches. This is especially appropriate in the study of kinship which, being in some ways the most technical aspect of anthropology, is also the aspect most open to the competition of a 'scientific' approach. But there is still a distinction between the study of culturally neutral scientific facts (the realm of the biologist) and the study of culturally specific social facts (the realm of the social anthropologist). Generally, the approach of the former cannot account for the variety of the latter.

Consider as an example the contrasting attitudes involved in the idea of a simple genealogy. An objective, scientific, biological genealogy for a particular human population is certainly conceivable if one can collect the necessary data. The social anthropologist knows that virtually any society will hold only a partial view of such a genealogy, emphasizing certain aspects (descent through a particular line, for example) and neglecting others (other potential modes of descent; *see further*, chapter 2), perhaps fabricating all or part of the genealogy for particular purposes, or even forgetting most of it after the lapse of a couple of generations. This in its turn affects the biologist in the sense that the collection of truly accurate genealogical data is made much more difficult, if not actually impossible, especially in societies that lack any written records. Like the social anthropologist, he or she is ultimately dependent on data collected from informants in a social context. Biologists may reply that the margin of error is insignificant, no worse than that which is found acceptable in scientific experiments generally, and that total accuracy is simply too much to expect. For many social anthropologists, however – for whom the cultural representation of biological facts is of more interest than the facts in themselves – this is enough to make the whole endeavour questionable, if not futile.

Yet conflict between the two disciplines is by no means inevitable. Social anthropologists should certainly not give way on the principle that biological universals can never explain the culturally specific, because the latter, by definition, exist only in particular societies and not universally. Nonetheless, they should recognize that very many, if not most, relations of kinship inescapably have a biological dimension, however they may be defined by the society concerned. Nor is all biology rigidly determinist: indeed, modern human biologists have become very interested in such things as the extent to which different social practices influence patterns of genetic relatedness. It must also be acknowledged that human biology has long since laid to rest the ghost of its past association with theories of race and the abuses they led to, even though these theories may linger in popular belief. The challenges posed to the anthropological study of kinship by other sciences with universalist claims, such as psychology and ethology, can be met in a broadly similar fashion. In that the latter are interested in establishing universals of thought and behaviour, cultural and social variation is not something they are easily equipped to deal with.

This brings us to the relationship between anthropology and science generally, and to the status of anthropology as a science. While its basic methodology need not be any less rigorous than that of the physical sciences, it is professionally well equipped to bring the values and practices of those sciences under sceptical scrutiny. Even the scientific world view forms a legitimate object of anthropological enquiry as regards its place in those societies that acknowledge it. Science has undoubtedly made great progress in understanding the physical world, and we can be confident that it will continue to do so; but this very expectation means that what science is able to give us is not complete and perfect knowledge for all time, but simply the state of knowledge *as it exists now*, that is, knowledge that is less perfect than it will be a year, ten years or a hundred years hence. In other words, the essentially Western scientific world view is no less partial and incomplete than non-Western world views, though for different reasons.

Even in Western societies, there are differences between this essentially scientific world view and the attitudes held by ordinary people. An example, one particularly relevant to the study of kinship, is the question of paternity. Western societies will recognize, where appropriate, that one's social father may not be one's genetic or physiological father. Yet establishing the difference in particular cases is ultimately not a matter of the correct use of science but of the acquisition of knowledge in a social context. Even Western science has encountered problems in proving physiological paternity in cases of doubt, meaning that the identity of the genetic father has been scientifically unknowable except, to some extent, through a process of elimination. The modern technique of DNA or genetic fingerprinting may seem greatly to have improved accuracy in these respects, but only specialists can be directly aware of the degree and nature of proof: the courts, who have to take such decisions, and the population at large have to take this on trust, unless they are prepared to carry out the necessary experiments to prove the matter for themselves. (In fact, even genetic finger-printing has increasingly come under legal challenge.) For the layperson in Western societies, therefore, knowledge of this sort is a matter of faith in experts, of belief engendered ultimately by an essentially socially determined attitude towards reason and science as superior to all other forms of knowledge. Elsewhere, different attitudes may prevail, and there may be no interest in, or realiza-tion of, scientific proof at all, so that kinship becomes even more evidently a matter of social definition, of belief. And the means of validating any belief itself constitutes a belief. Anthropologically, 'truth' is not the truth but whatever people in a particular society and/or set of circumstances decide is the truth: even in our own society, the two do not necessarily coincide. Ultimately, therefore, despite occasional scientific interventions, paternity, and kinship generally, remain matters of purely *social* definition.

Such considerations need not lead to an absolute cultural relativ-ism, but an overenthusiastic universalism is equally to be resisted. The range of different world views is impressive, an important consideration, because otherwise societies would barely be distin-guishable from one another at all, whether for themselves or for the anthropologist. But this is principally true of the most explicit and conscious level of data. Many aspects of social life are implicit, automatic and unconscious, felt rather than expressed, and there may be only a limited range of options open for expression. There is only a restricted number of ways of tracing descent from earlier generations, for instance, or of residence rules, or of viable marriage systems. Such aspects occur widely enough to invite comparative effort to establish cross-cultural correlations, but they are still not universal enough to rule out all cultural variation. Conscious, ex-plicit differences, however, may apply more particularly to situa-tions in which the society seeks to stress its own identity specifically. As far as kinship is concerned, we may find here: different ideas concerning parenthood, the relations between the sexes or the nature of marriage relations; particular symbols used to denote aspects of kinship; and different ways of rationalizing the existence of particular marriage or descent systems. These all promote variety rather than uniformity among cultures, and, at the level of greatest detail, they are likely to be culturally specific. At all events, cross-cultural correlations can only be built up carefully and piecemeal from data collected in the field; and, while theoretical hypotheses may lead the search for data, it is they that must ultimately give way in cases of conflict with it.

There is also the vexed question of the concepts and terms the anthropologist uses in discussions of kinship, and of the relationship between them, matters which are more or less the subject of this book. Anthropologists have not completely lacked imagination in developing concepts and terms specific to their subject. Nonetheless, they routinely use Western notions of kinship in describing indigenous representations of it, mainly to make them more readily understandable to themselves and to their readers. In the main, these are the notions of Western society rather than of Western science, though there is, of course, a degree of overlap between the two. This practice is part of the process of translation that anthropology is commonly felt to entail, and it means that the terms the anthropologist uses to describe and analyse kinship are themselves translations in this sense. They also represent abstractions, however, having been developed in the course of countless analyses, cross-cultural comparisons and discussions as to their significance and appropriateness. Anthropologists themselves are by no means in total agreement about how all these terms should be used, mainly because of the variety of cultural conceptions of kinship the terms have to deal with. Certainly these terms are grounded ultimately in ethnographic realities (in so far as these can be established correctly), but the point is that something is always lost in translation, a consequence of the very necessity of making the categories of one society understood in those of another.

This use of Western notions of kinship in discussions of non-Western ideas about it can never be more than a sort of shorthand device enabling rough-and-ready assessments to be made, and there is really no substitute for detailed descriptions of the particular indigenous world view that is being examined. Certainly, anthropology needs some sort of terminology in which to discuss its ideas; and because, as an academic discipline, it has traditionally been almost exclusively a part of the intellectual life of the West, it was inevitable that the West's terms and language should have been chosen for its discourse. But this is still a long way from the other, more questionable use sometimes made of Western ideas in anthropology, namely as the standard to which all other views of the world can, and must, be reduced. This attitude is the outcome of the idea that the Western world view is true, rational and scientific rather than just one world view among many, and of the notion that anthropology itself is a science like the natural sciences. Such views are unreflective on a number of counts: that a reduction of such data to a common standard distorts them in the very act of trying to simplify them; that the world view being scrutinized frequently lacks any idea of science in the Western sense, especially as something autonomous from other sorts of knowledge; and that for most contemporary anthropologists, science is itself a cultural object.

In the remainder of this work, therefore, the terms, and the concepts they label, are presented in the spirit of an anthropologist attracted neither by the despair of the cultural relativists nor by the pretensions of the scientific universalists. The aim is not to give absolute definitions, but to discuss how the terms are generally used by modern anthropologists and some of the problems associated with them. The concepts presented are therefore to be regarded not as features that all societies necessarily have nor as the basis for attempts to fit different societies into standard typologies. Rather, they are tools which help us describe more accurately particular indigenous world views and the circumstances of their existence.

Abbreviations and Diagrams

The study of kinship involves, among other things, the study of the relationships of any particular individual in the society, whether male or female. In discussing kinship systems, that individual is conventionally designated **ego** (in older works, often **Ego**). Sometimes, in discussing ego's relationships with just one other person, this other person is designated **alter** (**Alter**). A more generalized or collective term for the latter is **referent**. Abbreviations are available for different sorts of relative. There is a number of different systems:

I		II		III		IV	
F	father	Fa	father	F	father	F	father
M	mother	Mo	mother	m	mother	M	mother
B	brother	Br	brother	B	brother	B	brother
Z	sister	Si	sister	s	sister	S	sister
S	son	So	son	S	son	s	son
D	daughter	Da	daughter	d	daughter	d	daughter
H	husband	Hu	husband	H	husband	H	husband
W	wife	Wi	wife	w	wife	W	wife
P	parent	Pa	parent				
G	sibling	Sb	sibling				
E	spouse	Sp	spouse				
C	child	Ch	child				

The abbreviations in any one system are combined where necessary (for example, in II, FaSi = 'father's sister'). The first (I) is the one used in the rest of this book. It is nowadays the most usual in Europe, where even works in, for example, French and German tend to use this English-language convention (it is preferred in France because English word order conforms better than French to the tracing of genealogical paths outwards from ego to alter). To it can be added 'e' for 'elder' and 'y' for 'younger'; 'ms' for 'man speaking' (or 'male speaking') and 'ws' for 'woman speaking' (sometimes 'fs', 'female speaking'); and 'os' for 'opposite sex' and 'ss' for 'same sex'. 'e', 'y', 'os' and 'ss' are normally placed before the symbol to which they relate. When in final position, however, 'e' and 'y' refer to the whole specification. For example, eB = 'elder brother'; MeBD = 'mother's elder brother's daughter'; MeBDy = 'a mother's elder brother's daughter who is younger than ego' [MeByD could mean only 'mother's elder brother's younger daughter (of two or more daughters)']. Purists argue that because B is itself a whole specification, the abbreviation for 'elder brother' should logically read Be. Against this, eB has the advantage of adhering to English word order, and the qualifying 'e' still obeys the rule of appearing *before* the symbol to which it relates.

The use of symbols indicating alter's sex relative to ego ('os' and 'ss') is similar. An example is the formula PssG, meaning 'parent's same-sex sibling', that is, mother's sister and father's brother (if, for example, they have the same kin term). PGss would mean a parent's sibling who was of the same gender as *ego*. In the case of 'ms' and 'ws' (or 'fs'), the choice of where the symbols go is less critical, because there is less possibility of misunderstanding. For example, MBDms and msMBD both stand for 'a male ego's mother's brother's daughter' (for example, in the case of a term *not* used by a female). Both formulas are found, though in practice there is a marked preference for the former, in which 'ms' comes after the genealogical specification.

The last four lines of I and II each provides a set of sex-neutral symbols as an alternative to the sex-specific ones above them. II is an American system, slowly giving way to I. III uses small letters for females, IV for juniors; both also of American origin, they have now largely fallen out of use but may be encountered in older works. Yet other systems may occasionally be encountered (Russian anthropology has its own Levine system), but they tend to be specific to particular authors and we need not dwell on them here.

Each of the above abbreviations, whether single or in combination, can be seen as a symbol standing for a particular kin type. A kin type such as FB (father's brother) is not generally equivalent to just one position on a genealogy (ego's father may have more than one brother or none at all), nor to an indigenous category within a kinship terminology that is isolated from other categories through a particular kin term. For example, FB may have the same term as MB, as in English, or alternatively the same term as MZH (*see further*, chapters 5–7). Of course, there are exceptions. For example, the notion of father (F) does frequently combine kin type, genealogical position and category-term; but equally there are cases where ego's mother has more than one husband and/or where the term for 'father' is also applied to his brothers and perhaps to ego's MZH too. A kin type is therefore in principle an analytical concept, not an indigenous one. At the indigenous level, one encounters rather a set of categories, each identifiable by kin term.

Diagrams are often used in discussing kinship (*see* Figs. 1.1 and 1.2). These frequently, but not invariably, use the conventions of the genealogy. Male individuals are represented by triangles, female individuals by circles; sometimes a rectangle (square or diamond shaped) is used to denote individuals regardless of their sex. Sometimes ♂ stands for male and ♀ for female. Ego may (but not always) be represented by a solid symbol. Conversely, this may denote a deceased individual, though these are more usually represented by the appropriate symbol 'cancelled' with a diagonal line or slash. These symbols may stand for groups as well as for individuals: for example, the males of one generation in a particular descent group (*see* chapter 2).

Relationships between individuals are shown by lines or other symbols. Connections by descent or filiation are indicated by vertical lines (sometimes slanted or staggered if the diagram requires it). Siblingship is indicated by raised horizontal lines. Marriage is indicated by lowered horizontal lines or by the equals sign (=), though the latter is also used in discussing kinship terminologies (*see* chapter 5) either (1) to translate kin terms (e.g. *nam* = MBD), or (2) to denote the sharing of a single kin term by more than one separate kin type (e.g. MB = WF; conversely, the symbol ≠ denotes lack of terminological equivalence). A loop is used to carry lines over one another where they are not intended to be conceived as intersecting or joining. The order of generations in the diagram proceeds, as might be expected, down the page. If age order is significant in respect of a group of siblings or other members of the same generation, then the order of descending seniority normally follows a left-right order across the page.

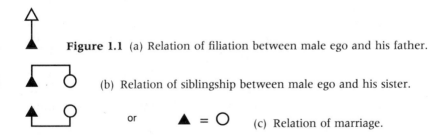

Figure 1.1 (a) Relation of filiation between male ego and his father.

(b) Relation of siblingship between male ego and his sister.

or ▲ = ○   (c) Relation of marriage.

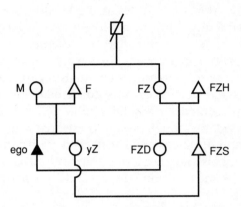

Figure 1.2 Symbols. The diagram shows male ego's marriage to his FZD, and that of his yZ to his FZS (who is younger than FZD). Everyone of this generation, plus ego's F and FZ, are descended from a deceased individual of unspecified sex. Ego's parents' generation also shows two marriages.

Such diagrams may be used to show any one of a number of different things:

1 an actual **genealogy**, that is, the ways in which real living or deceased individuals are said to be related to one another in the society in question (genealogies may nonetheless include mythical figures or be partly fabricated from our point of view);
2 the model of a particular **kinship system** or a part of it (for example, marriage system, descent system), that is, the way in which representative individuals, or organized and defined groups of individuals (for example, descent groups, alliance groups – *see* chapters 2 and 4), are typically or ideally related to one another in a particular society;
3 the content of such relationships or a particular subsidiary aspect of them or of the system (for example, the circulation of gifts among particular kin types);
4 abstractions or models of kinship systems made by the anthropologist on the basis of features that are more or less common to a number of societies (for example, bilateral cross-cousin marriage – *see* chapter 6);

5 the kinship terminology, though many anthropologists prefer other ways of representing this diagramatically (*see* chapter 5).

The exact purpose of any particular diagram should always be made clear by the writer and ascertained by the reader to avoid confusion between the various possibilities. Diagrams are only *representations* of reality using arbitrary conventions and symbols: they have to be read properly to be understood properly.

In effect, diagrams are generally expressions either of real events and situations, or else of some sort of **model**. It should be obvious that most of these models are analytical ones that have been put together by the anthropologist on the basis of indigenous views and statements, but which are also abstractions and will probably reflect the anthropologist's theoretical interests. The aim may be precisely to give a model of some aspect of kinship in a specific society, whether of indigenous values or of either actual or typical behaviour. This is basically the familiar distinction between ideal and real, between indigenous theory and practice. Conversely, the purpose of the model may be comparative, that is, to represent some aspect of kinship typical of a range of societies (examples have in effect already been given in the previous paragraph). It is worth remembering, however, that it is also possible to talk of indigenous models – sometimes called **folk models** – that is, those held by the members of the particular society being studied. These, of course, are liable to be set in quite different terms from those of the academic analyst, being perhaps more informal and less structured, probably emphasizing ideals rather than facts. It is one anthropological task to ensure that such models are translated into terms understandable by one's colleagues and students – hence the need, once again, for an adequate terminology. Unless otherwise stated, the word 'model' will always denote 'analytical model', not 'folk model', in the rest of this work.

2
Descent

Every child, by the fact of his or her birth, is normally recognized to be related to at least one parent, and usually, but not invariably, to both. Even where both are recognized, the quality of the child's relationship to each of its parents may be conceived to differ. For instance, the father need not be recognized as contributing to pregnancy or to birth at all; alternatively, he may be regarded as responsible for the one but not the other – simply 'opening the way' for the child to be born, for example. Conversely, the mother may be the sole agent in the creation of a new life, or merely the vessel in which the father plants his seed. Finally, other powers – spirits, gods, ancestors, even other living individuals – may be deemed to be involved as well as the parents.

Anthropologists use the terms **pater** and **mater** to indicate the socially defined father and mother respectively, in contradistinction to the physical or biological father and mother, the **genitor** and **genetrix**. This may not always be followed indigenously, for example, where the society makes no clear distinction between the two, or in stories of virgin births and the like, which may reverse them. As we have already seen (chapter 1), the identification even of the physical parents is an essentially *social* definition that need not be interpreted in exactly the same way in every society. Thus strictly speaking, the genitor/genetrix should be distinguished also from the genetic parents as Western science would identify them even though, in very many instances, the two can be regarded as identical. This takes into account the fact that instead of the scientific definition, many societies will have their own view of what constitutes 'real parenthood' as distinct from 'social parenthood', a remark which applies to concepts of relatedness in general.

In whatever way they are recognized, these simple links between parent and child are ties of **filiation**, sometimes specified further as **patrifiliation** (between father and child) and **matrifiliation** (between mother and child). Often, it is only these ties that are important indigenously. However, filiation links are repeated generation after generation, and if the social emphasis is on the whole series of such links, backwards into preceding generations and, prospectively, forwards into future ones, then one talks of **descent**. French *filiation* unhappily refers to both 'filiation' and 'descent'.

Descent does not take the same form everywhere, and may not even be recognized at all. Very often, links traced through one parent are emphasized at the expense, relatively or absolutely, of those through the other. If links through the father are emphasized, there is **patrilineal** or **agnatic descent**; if links through the mother are emphasized, there is **matrilineal** or **uterine descent**. In both cases, descent is **unilineal**, the **descent line** formed by these links being traced back in time through persons of the same sex to the ancestor or founder of the line (often a mythical figure; *see* Fig. 2.1). One frequently encounters three of the above terms as nouns (**patriliny, agnation, matriliny**), and the suffix '-lineal' occasionally occurs in the form **-linear** ('matrilinear' etc.).

Usually, *all* children born to the line, regardless of their sex, will in unilineal descent be attached to it through the appropriate parent (father or mother, that is, F > C; M > C). But only the lineally stressed children (sons with patrilineal descent, daughters with matrilineal descent) will continue the line (that is, F > S; M > D). In other words, unilineal descent typically gives status to children of both genders, but only those of one gender will transmit descent further into future generations. Each son or daughter may (as appropriate, and given children of their own) form lines of their own, through branching. From the point of view of any one line, the other lines are **collateral** lines of descent. One such line (for example, that of the eldest or youngest child of the lineally stressed sex) may be recognized as pre-eminent (especially with regard to

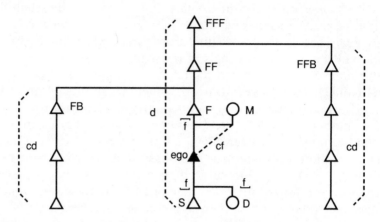

Figure 2.1 Descent and filiation. The figure shows patrilineal descent in male ego's own line (d), his collateral lines of patrilineal descent (cd), and his ties of filiation (f) and complementary filiation (cf). In this case, filiation is with the father, complementary filiation with the mother; they would be reversed were descent matrilineal.

inheritance or succession; *see below*), though this need not be the case.

Unilineal descent does not rule out the recognition of relationships with relatives who are not related to ego in this way; it simply gives a certain priority to those who are. The connection between a child of either sex and the other, non-lineally stressed parent (the mother with patrilineal descent, the father with matrilineal descent) has been called **complementary filiation** (*see* Fig. 2.1). Some anthropologists stress complementary filiation because it forms the connecting link between the child and the descent line or descent group (*see below*) of the non-lineally stressed parent (for example, of the mother in a society with patrilineal descent). Others would argue, however, that these links really depend on the *marriage* of the child's parents and should be treated as such. Ego's links in general to one or both parents or through them to his or her lines of descent, however identified, are sometimes called (**ties of**) **affiliation** (not to be confused with filiation, which is restricted to links between ego and the parents specifically).

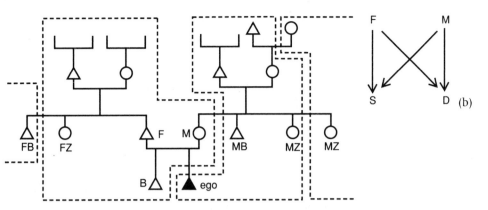

Figure 2.2 (a) Cognatic descent. The dotted lines enclose different residential groups; they represent only one set of possibilities among many. This example shows ego's parents residing together with his brother, but ego himself residing with his MB; similarly, ego's two mother's sisters live separately from one another and from ego's mother, as does ego's FB.
(b) Ties of cognatic descent between two siblings of opposite sex and their parents.

Patrilineal and matrilineal descent emphasize links through one sex only. In some societies, no stress is put on one of these lines at the expense of the other; both are given equal importance, and an individual traces his or her descent through both parents indifferently. Descent in such cases is **bilateral** or **cognatic** (sometimes **ambilateral**, **ambilineal** or **non-unilineal**; in French also *indifférencié*; *see* Fig. 2.2).

Any mode of descent may arrange those individuals linked by it into **descent groups**, although these are by no means found everywhere, and even where they do occur, they rarely control everything in the society and may never meet as a group. Indeed, descent may well be recognized without groups being formed from it, which has led some anthropologists to distinguish **descent constructs** or **descent categories** (that is, the ideological recognition of descent ties) from the formation of descent groups proper.

Unilineal descent groups are regularly called **clans** or **lineages**, depending on their vertical depth. Conventionally, lineages are descent groups which are shallow enough for the links between all their members to be known and traceable. Clans are of deeper extent, beyond the limits of such knowledge, and unilineal descent groups especially are typically descended from a mythical, not a living or recently deceased ancestor, nor even a historical one in many cases (though the people themselves may not be bothered by such niceties). In much earlier, especially American writing, the term **sib** is used as an alternative for clan. This arose out of an even earlier usage in which the term 'clan' was restricted to matrilineal descent groups, while **gens**, plural **gentes**, was used for patrilineal ones. This necessitated recourse to 'sib' as an umbrella term covering both, which itself later became subject to qualification as **patrisib** or **matrisib**. Such usages have now been completely superseded but deserve to be remembered to avoid confusion when reading older works. The use by historians of the word 'clan' for groups that are not really formed through recognizable descent ties at all has long been avoided in anthropology (for example, for what are basically administrative units or the assemblies of a chief's political supporters).

Clans are sometimes specified further as **patriclans** or **matriclans**, lineages rather more often as **patrilineages** or **matrilineages**. Lineages are also sometimes characterized as **maximal** or **minimal, major** or **minor**, and so on , according to relative size, and the term **segment** may also be used (and characterized similarly) of any lower-order grouping of either clan or lineage. A descent group is indeed **segmentary**, that is it consists of a number of co-ordinate branches which are all collateral lines (*see above*) to one another. Descent groups may be either localized in one community or dispersed in several, and there may be more than one in any single community. A segment that is also a residential unit or localized in some other sense is sometimes called a **local descent group**.

Cognatic descent groups are sometimes called **demes** or **ramages**, though, on occasion, the latter is also used of unilineal descent groups, in which case it generally suggests that the segments are ranked hierarchically. Sometimes **conical clan** is used in this latter sense, because segments at the top of the hierarchy will be less numerous or extensive than those at the bottom (and may also be endogamous, that is restricting or disallowing out-marriage; *see below*). The term **sept** has also been used to denote unilineal and, perhaps more usually, cognatic descent groups, but it is old-fashioned and now entirely redundant. Indigenously, descent groups may be unnamed or (especially if unilineal) named after an emblem (or **totem**, often something naturally occurring, though this need not be concerned with descent at all), the ancestor (who is then the **eponymous** ancestor), a locality, and so on. Ancestral figures need not be of the gender suggested by the descent line: there are many examples of patrilineal descent groups which trace their descent from an ancestress.

A basic distinction is often made between unilineal descent groups and cognatic ones, not merely because of their respective modes of descent, but also because of the different characteristics that are attributed to them. Thus a unilineal descent group is frequently thought of as being: **exogamous**, that is, as requiring or tending to have its members marry outside it; discrete, its boundaries being defined by its exogamy; of narrow lateral extent (beyond a certain point, collateral lines will break away and form new descent groups); and with definite preferences as to residence (*see* chapter 3). A cognatic descent group, on the other hand, is often regarded as being: amorphous; of wider lateral extent; with overlapping membership; and usually **endogamous** (that is, as requiring or tending to have its members marry within it). This is because societies with cognatic descent groups often allow membership or other claims to be maintained with respect to more than one such group simultaneously, whether permanently or temporarily.

Accordingly, it is often argued that residence rather than descent is really the key criterion for membership in cognatic descent groups, as distinct from unilineal ones. The degree of choice typically allowed the individual as regards both membership and residence has also led some anthropologists to exclude the cognatic mode of descent from descent proper. This is because they regard descent as something uniquely and permanently determined for ego by his or her birth (and not by residence as such), something which would give any descent group an exact criterion for membership and therefore definite boundaries, without overlapping with other groups of the same kind. In this view, descent is seen as properly a characteristic of the unilineal modes only, which supposedly give ego no choice in the matter. Another objection occasionally made is that only filiation, not descent, is truly cognatic or bilateral.

While there is some truth in these characterizations in respect of many societies, they are too sweeping to be generally applicable. First, the idea that ego can exploit claims in as many cognatic descent groups as he or she can trace links with conflicts with the notion that cognatic descent groups are generally endogamous: in the latter case, ego and most of his or her relatives will belong to the same group, thus limiting ego's links with other such groups. Secondly, unilineal descent groups may also be endogamous, either at all levels of segmentation or at just the highest level (a clan might not be as strictly exogamous as the lineages into which it is divided). Conversely, even quite large cognatic descent groups may be exogamous, and even a basically endogamous cognatic descent group will normally have some exogamous boundaries within it, if only around the immediate family.

Thirdly, unilineal descent groups do not invariably exclude the exercise of choice as to either membership or residence among a number of such units ego might be able to claim links with. Ego may be able to make claims through his or her collateral ties with other segments of the same descent group, or through ties of marriage or complementary filiation with other descent groups of the same type (that is, they are still basically unilineal, not cognatic, despite the possible exploitation of links through complementary filiation (cf. Fig. 3.3). For instance, a male ego in certain societies with patrilineal descent groups may choose to live and work in the patrilineal descent group of his mother or wife (and therefore of his MB or WF), or in a different collateral segment of his own patrilineal descent group (for example, the segment of a cousin related to him through his father, FF, FFF etc.). With unilineal as with cognatic descent, therefore, descent *per se* may receive less emphasis than residence as the key criterion for membership, especially if descent ties proper are recognized or remembered only two or three generations back. Lastly, even where there is not this degree of choice, egos of the non-lineally stressed sex may have acknowledged ties with two unilineal descent groups of the same type, that of birth and that of marriage.

Once these considerations are taken into account, the differences between unilineal and cognatic descent and descent groups in terms other than mode of descent diminish, rendering less objectionable the treatment of the latter as true descent. There are certainly borderline cases, and this is where the theoretical tendencies of the ethnographer may make themselves felt. For example, descent groups which are definable as cognatic on the basis of indigenous ideals may in practice stress unilineal (especially, perhaps, agnatic) links for some or most purposes. It can only be a matter of judgement sometimes as to whether one is really dealing with a situation of this sort or with a case of basically agnatic descent groups allowing a large measure of recruitment through non-agnatic links. The latter situation often seems to occur where genealogical memory is very shallow, so that recruitment is seen as a matter of filiation (that is, links with a parent) rather than descent.

Descent groups of any sort have a tendency to split over time, as they become larger and more dispersed, or if no attempt is made to maintain genealogical or other knowledge concerning membership. Sometimes, such splits are brought about deliberately to accommodate a marriage that would otherwise break exogamous rules. Other socially defined entities may be exogamous or endogamous, according to the society (often a tendency rather than a rigid rule), for example, the village community. Yet other institutions tend more definitely to be endogamous, for example: religious communities; elite groups in a socially stratified society; Indian castes; and often the ethnic group taken as a whole. In cases where the rule of endogamy of such a group has been broken through mixed marriages, the children are often attributed to the mother's group, even where descent as such is not matrilineal. If such marriages take place frequently, a new and probably endogamous group may be formed. Endogamous groups are themselves frequently divided into exogamous units (for example, clans within an Indian caste): endogamous boundaries must always fall more widely than exogamous ones.

Although there is much variation in theory and in practice, the term 'descent' is best reserved for **recruitment** by birth into, and membership of, descent groups where they occur, and more generally to the nature of the particular recognition given to ego's vertical ties in defining his or her own status. This usage also stresses the continuity of descent between succeeding generations. Descent is sometimes defined directly as the holding of property and office and their transmission between generations, the descent group then often being considered a 'moral person' or 'corporation' (the **corporate descent group**), which never dies and whose members have specific rights and duties in relation to it and/or their fellow members. Certainly, any mode of descent can be used for the transmission of things and attributes from generation to generation, and it is unusual for descent groups to exist in and of themselves, devoid of other purpose. But it is not in fact the case that descent groups are everywhere property or office holding – they may, for example, simply regulate marriage through their exogamy.

Descent as defined above should therefore be distinguished analytically from **inheritance** (of property, which may include the intangible, such as a name or spiritual essence) and from **succession** (to office, including ritual office). One reason for making these distinctions is that although the same modes may be used in inheritance and succession, and the same terms (patrilineal, matrilineal, cognatic, etc.) used to describe them, not everything is necessarily transmitted in the same mode in any one society: for instance, property may devolve cognatically, office patrilineally. Moreover, as we have seen, descent as a form of *recruitment* normally applies to individuals of both sexes in the society, regardless of the nature of the links used for its onward transmission to later generations: in other words, even where there is unilineal descent, so that only children of one gender will be responsible for the further continuity of the line of descent, all individuals receive status through descent at birth. Unilineal inheritance and succession, on the other hand, make a radical distinction between the sexes. For example, the fact that the children of both sexes are recruited to a patrilineal descent group by birth (that is, $F > C$) logically conflicts with the fact that even where inheritance and succession are also patrilineal, male children will benefit, either relatively or (especially in the case of succession) absolutely (that is, $F > S$).

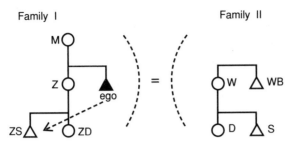

Figure 2.3 The matrilineal family. There are actually two, organized around opposite-sex sibling links, not a married couple. Male ego is in one, his wife and children in the other. The pecked arrow shows the path of inheritance or succession between male ego and his ZS with matrilineal descent.

The situation with matrilineal inheritance and succession is more complicated, in that both often proceed between males, though *via* females. For example, succession to office may proceed from mother's brother to sister's son matrilineally, the link being provided by a woman who is simultaneously the sister of the former and the mother of the latter, without she herself acquiring the office (*see* Fig. 2.3). Here, therefore, although we can represent descent by M > C, succession and/or inheritance may have to be represented by MB > ZS. Similarly, patrilineal inheritance and succession may give a preference for a younger brother over a son (yielding eB > yB). The level of segmentation is also significant in establishing what, if anything, descent does. For example, the clan may regulate marriage, the lineages into which it is divided being perhaps units of inheritance or of joint ritual activity. These examples show that it is rarely appropriate to characterize a whole society in terms of any particular mode of descent, for example, as 'patrilineal' or 'matrilineal' or 'cognatic', despite a widespread tendency to do so.

Even where different attributes or sorts of property are transmitted by each of the two unilineal modes separately, many societies nonetheless have only one sort of unilineal descent group (for example, even in a society with only patrilineal descent groups, female clothes and ornaments may be inherited matrilineally), while others may lack descent groups entirely. Yet other societies have both sorts of unilineal descent group, one patrilineal, the other matrilineal. Such societies are frequently described as having **bilineal** or **double unilineal descent**, the latter expression being used mostly by those who see descent primarily as a matter of the transmission of property rather than simply of acknowledged vertical ties or group membership. More accurately, however, it is a matter of the co-presence of both sorts of unilineal descent or unilineal descent group (patrilineal *and* matrilineal) in the same society, whatever further purposes they might fulfil. In such cases, the assumption generally is that children of *both* sexes are equally recruited at birth into *both* the unilineal lines or groups of descent, regardless of any differences in rights or status that may arise subsequently between sons and daughters: that is, recruitment is a matter of $F > C + M > C$, while continuity of line into the following generations is a matter of $F > S + M > D$ (cf. unilineal descent, above). Another way of distinguishing such cases from unilineal descent is by reference to ego's descent links with his or her various grandparents. In unilineal descent, only FF (with patrilineal descent) or MM (with matrilineal descent) are linked by descent to ego; in bilineal or double unilineal descent, on the other hand, *both* are so linked. 'Bilineal' or 'double unilineal' ($F > C + M > C$) should not be confused with 'ambilineal' or '(am)bilateral' or 'cognatic' (that is, $F/M > C$). Although it is an authentic form, not all attempts to identify two different lines of unilineal descent have been credible, especially where one of these has to be considered 'submerged', 'hidden' or 'implicit' (*see further, below*; also chapter 6).

In those rarely reported and rather uncertain cases where not only continuity of line but also recruitment to the two lines or groups are said to be more absolutely sex-specific ($F > S + M > D$ in both cases), one talks of **parallel descent**. There are also a very few societies in which descent is reported to be **alternating**, that is, it proceeds from male to female in one generation and from female to male in the next. Not all societies recognize descent in the sense of links between *successive* generations: in some, recruitment skips a generation, so that ego enters the **section** of a grandparent (*see further*, chapter 6). Inheritance too may skip a generation, for example, the transmission of name and soul from grandparent to grandchild (*see* Fig. 2.4).

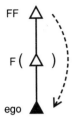

Figure 2.4 Patrilineal links skipping a generation.

Inheritance or succession by the eldest child is **primogeniture**, by the youngest **ultimogeniture**. Inheritance can be either **pre-mortem** or **post-mortem**, that is, it takes place respectively before or after the death of whomever one inherits from. It should be remembered that much property regularly comes into and goes out of a family or descent group through marriage ties rather than as inheritance, although indigenously this distinction may be blurred (*see further*, chapter 4). As for office, this may be acquired by election or co-option on the basis of personality, ability, wealth, and so on, and not necessarily by hereditary succession at all.

Descent should also be distinguished from authority, despite the use of **patriarchal** and **matriarchal** in some very old works to suggest descent, a confused usage which is now entirely redundant. This is particularly significant in respect of any society with matrilineal descent, in which, despite the emphasis on female links, men very often control affairs, though often as brothers and maternal uncles rather than as husbands and fathers (as it is more usual to expect in societies with patrilineal descent). Conversely, societies with patrilineal descent by no means invariably deny all authority and influence to women, though this may be limited to particular spheres – most frequently, perhaps, the household, but also ritual, market trading, and so on. The revival of 'patriarchal' and 'matriarchal' in some modern feminist-oriented anthropology is mostly confined to denoting authority and modes of domination. Longer-established alternatives in these senses are **patripotestal** and **matripotestal**.

Finally, descent should be distinguished from **residence rules**, which are often characterized by similar though not identical names (*see further*, chapter 3). One reason is that so-called residence 'rules' are likely to be more flexible in practice than rules of descent, and so on. But again, the principal reason is that there is no necessary correlation between residence rules and descent, inheritance or succession. Although descent frequently has a territorial dimension, persons linked by descent may be territorially dispersed, and ties of co-residence that do not involve descent may be more important. Indeed, many anthropologists go further and see territoriality, that is, common residence, as more important than descent, even as replacing it entirely. Although certainly appropriate in particular cases, these views do not present a challenge to the notion of descent in general. A variant of these approaches is the suggestion that co-residence is itself the basis of descent, that is, people do not live together because they are related by descent but are related by descent because they live together. Certainly if descent in a society has a high degree of residential compactness, descent and residence are necessarily going to be closely intertwined; by the same token, however, one can hardly give a logical priority to either in such cases. In any case, this situation is far from being invariable. Thanks to the frequent dispersal of descent groups, descent and residence can be distinguished, not just analytically, but frequently ethnographically as well.

The exact nature of descent and its concomitants in any particular society can nonetheless be very hard to determine, even where it is recognized to exist. Given the necessary genealogical knowledge, the anthropologist could in theory trace descent groups of any mode throughout any society he or she happened to be studying. However, while some anthropologists have occasionally tried to suggest the presence of lines of 'implicit' or 'hidden' descent for specific purposes (*see* above, *also* chapter 6), the approach is essentially a false one. It is certain that any society will recognize only some of the possibilities open to it, and it is these, that is, what is indigenously recognized, that a social anthropologist, as distinct from a biologist, should seek to isolate and analyse.

As a professional academic notion, descent has certainly suffered a degree of reification in the past, to the extent that anthropologists have sometimes imagined it rather than identified it in the field. This does not render it useless, for there are still many societies which give it importance. Whether or not it does feature in the collective ideas of the people being studied – and if so, the actual form it takes – are questions that always have to be determined independently. Genealogical memory may be very shallow, extending back only two or three generations at most, and as a mode of recruitment to social groups, filiation ties with one or both parents may be stressed more than links with a long line of probably partly fictitious ancestors. Social groups are often defined not through descent but through common residence, property holding, unity in conducting marriage alliances, effective political or social action, co-operation in economic activities, possessing a common name, gift exchange, partaking in a common ritual (which may in part be directed towards the group's ancestors), and so on. It may also be the proper discharge of marriage payments (*see* chapter 4), not descent, that is decisive in determining group membership for the children born to a marriage. Note that none of these attributes can be either explained by, or assimilated to, any biological notions. A human biologist may well regard ties of descent and consanguinity as in principle unending and never broken, because of the unity of the human species. Any society, however, even in the West, will set a definite and quite narrow limit to any descent it recognizes, not least because it will often regard itself as the only truly human society.

3
The Family and Other Kir Groupings

The Family

While descent groups are structures of often considerable extent, at the minimal level one will normally be able to identify some type of **family**, and sometimes this is all a society will recognize by way of kin grouping. Ideas of the family tend to vary not only from society to society but also from author to author, some definitions using composition or membership as the criterion, others function; those ethnographic descriptions that combine the two are likely to be the most useful. The term **household** is freely used as a synonym of 'family' by some authors, while others use it to mark some variation in structure, such as a grouping of lower or higher order. 'Household' always implies the notion of co-residence, however, which 'family' need not.

Strictly, a **nuclear** or **elementary** or **conjugal family** consists merely of parents and children, though it often includes one or two other relatives as well, for example, a widowed parent or unmarried sibling of one or other spouse. A **stem family** links the nuclear family of one married child with his or her natal family.

The nuclear family has often been claimed to be the very foundation of all human society, but not all societies actually give it this particular emphasis. Indeed, families may easily be more extensive, perhaps taking the form of an **extended family** or a **joint family**. Theoretically, the former consists of members of three or more generations, perhaps with some collateral branching (that is, has vertical extension), while the latter consists of the nuclear families of a number of siblings or same-generation cousins (that is, has horizontal extension). In practice, however, such groupings tend to be quite fluid in composition and may have both characteristics. This often depends on the position they have reached in their cycle of development. An extended family will change into a joint family with the death of the oldest generation, provided it survives that event, while a nuclear family will develop into an extended family if the children of the original pair remain at home after marrying and having children themselves. Generally, however, even large families tend to have a limited existence compared to a descent group which, in principle, can continue forever. Extended and joint families are often identified further as patrilineal, matrilineal, bilateral, cognatic, and so on, if the links between the generations are regularly structured in such ways. The term 'extended family' or something similar may refer indigenously to a series of families which are connected by ties of kinship, without any implication of co-residence.

The family is not necessarily the property-holding unit: this may be a wider descent group or a narrower group of relatives or simply the individual. Nor is the family necessarily the domestic unit in the sense of the unit which eats, sleeps and works together: several 'families' (however defined) may form one domestic unit; a single joint or extended family may consist of more than one domestic unit; and the domestic unit may exclude or lack one parent or other relative, at least at times. One example of the latter is the **matrifocal family**, a common phenomenon in some parts of the world where adult males regularly leave home for long periods to work or for some other purpose. Another, of course, is the essentially modern, Western concept of the one-parent family. It is often difficult to identify any particular type of family with any particular society, because the births, marriages and deaths of family members inevitably change the composition of any family through a repetitive process of fission and fusion.

Families may be **polygynous** or **polyandrous** (**polygamous**; see Chapter 4), that is, consist of a man or woman with more than one spouse and corresponding sets of children, though often each co-spouse may form a separate household with his or, more often, her children. One can also distinguish one's **natal family** or **family of orientation**, the family into which one is born, from one's **family of procreation**, the family one creates through, and following, one's marriage. The difference in perspective is between that of a child and that of a spouse, so that the same family can be both to different kin types.

Sometimes ego may, whether temporarily or permanently, be a member of other families than these, whether through **fostering (fosterage)** or **adoption**. Fostering is usually reserved for temporary situations which do not affect the status of the person being fostered in the long term, especially a temporary sojourn with a close relative to help with a child's upbringing in a general sense. Because this may be regarded as providing spiritual as well as physical nurture, it is frequently seen as something desirable rather than a necessary response to a situation of crisis in the original family. Adoption, on the other hand, is usually seen as involving a permanent alteration of status for the adoptee. Ego may be adopted for his or her own sake (for example, because he or she is an orphan needing care) or to provide an heir and/or successor where none has become available through the means normal in the society (such as the failure of the adopter to acquire a legitimate son through normal procreative means). Obviously, the two very often go together, because the adoptee's poverty may drive him or her into such an arrangement. Where inheritance is an issue, there may be a preference for adopting someone within, for example, the same descent group (such as a brother's son in a society with landholding patrilineal descent groups), so that the property involved remains in the clan despite the adoption. Sometimes, a part of the bargain is that a male ego marries the daughter of his adopter, in which case (again given patrilineal descent) his own son, though the daughter's son of the adopter, will continue the latter's line (*see* Fig. 3.1). Such marriages are rarely regarded as more than a necessary makeshift in the societies concerned.

In some, but by no means all, societies with matrilineal descent, the family nucleus consists not of husband and wife (or, from the point of view of the following generation, father and mother) but of brother and sister (or mother's brother and mother); a man eats

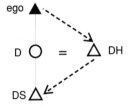

Figure **3.1** Patrilineal inheritance through adopted DH (via pecked lines).

and works at his natal home with his own sister and *her* children, though visiting his wife nightly, whose household is also that of his own children and his wife's brother (*see* Fig. 2.3). An alternative type of **matrilineal family** consists of a number of husbands living in a subordinate position in the extended family of their wives' MB or of some other affine.

From this, we see that residence rules vary considerably from society to society. The residence of a person or household in the natal home, village, and so on, of the husband is called **patrilocal** or, better, **virilocal** (sometimes **patrivirilocal**). Residence in the natal home, village, and so on, of the wife is called **matrilocal** or, better, **uxorilocal**. The reason for preferring the second term in each case is that these more literally suggest residence at a place associated specifically with the husband or wife respectively. The first term in each pair literally suggests that husband and wife are also parents, which will not always be the case, especially early in the marriage. In practice, these two terms are perhaps more often thought of as focusing on the respective same-sex *parents* of the couple, patrilocal referring to residence with the husband's father, matrilocal to residence with the wife's mother. Both these terms suffer from their obvious linguistic formation on 'patrilineal' and 'matrilineal' respectively.

If there is no definite rule, and residence can be in the home or village of either spouse, then the term **ambilocal** is used (occasionally **utrolocal**, if a choice is possible but cannot easily be altered once made). If it is desired to stress that residence is to be in a new location or house, then the term **neolocal** is appropriate. **Natolocal** refers to residence in the house or village of one's birth, which, taken literally, can usually only describe the situation for one spouse, especially if the reference is to a house. **Duolocal** residence refers to separate residence by husband and wife. In a few societies, ego lives for a time or permanently in the village, home, and so on, of a maternal uncle, in which case residence for him or her is **avunculocal**. A counterpart, of residence with the paternal aunt, is sometimes identified under the term **amitalocal**, though ethnographic instances are scarcely known. Residence is not necessarily uniform either throughout the life cycle or throughout the society, and should often be seen as a matter of preferences or mere tendencies rather than hard and fast rules.

Other Kin Groupings

Whatever other characteristics they may have, descent groups are invariably ancestor focused, that is, they consist of the line or lines that *descend* from the real or mythical ancestor or founder, often called the **apical** ancestor or founder (from 'apex'): if one were to trace all the lines back, they would converge on the ancestor. Descent groups are therefore to be distinguished from the **kindred**, which is often considered ego focused, but more accurately consists of all those kin who are connected through specific ties with ego and his or her siblings (*see* Fig. 3.2). No two sibling groups will have exactly the same kindred, though there will be much overlapping (by contrast, many sibling groups will share a descent group of sufficient depth). Kindreds usually recognize male and female links, that is, they are cognatic, though there are some rare examples of unilineal ones. Kindreds need not be bounded by genealogical distance but by geographical distance, or generation or some other social factor. More distant links may be assumed rather than demonstrated, and, as with cognatic descent groups, their boundaries may be fuzzy. Relatives by marriage may be included, though some kindreds are exogamous. Others are preferentially endogamous within particular boundaries (for example, excluding the nuclear family), a circumstance which tends to reduce their range by duplicating the possible genealogical links between ego and certain alters.

Kindreds often have some specific purpose, which as well as the

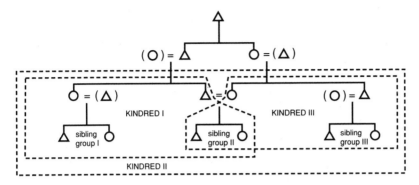

Figure 3.2 The kindred. The diagram shows the bilateral kindreds of three different sibling groups; affines are excluded (though this is not a necessary feature). The whole diagram can be seen as a bilateral descent group, descended from the male in the senior generation. Sibling group II is the focus of the largest kindred (II); only this group are members of all three kindreds.

regulation of marriage may be economic co-operation, help in feuding, and so on. They may become apparent only when this purpose is invoked, especially as they are often unnamed. Because they are focused on a sibling group, kindreds have much less continuity over time than the typical descent group – indeed, they die out with the last member of the focal sibling group. In some early texts, the kindred is defined as a bilateral descent group, but the above definition is now standard.

Descent can be thought of as the chronological or vertical dimension of kinship, and the term **generation** distinguishes phases in the chronology. This distinction is, of course, an arbitrary one, in the sense that people are being born and dying continually, and not just every 30 years or so. The term also tends to denote people of the same age rather than those who should be grouped together horizontally by genealogy. It is therefore better to use the term **genealogical level** in the latter sense (in some societies, for example, relatives who fall into the same kin category as ego's genealogical uncle may commonly be of approximately the same age as ego or younger, even though they belong to a different level of the genealogy). In analyses, ego's level is usually numbered 0 (zero; sometimes called the **level of reference**), that of his or her parents

+1, that of the grandparents +2, that of the children −1, that of the grandchildren −2, and so on. This order is occasionally reversed (especially in French writings), so that the senior generations are designated with the negative sign, the junior generations with the positive sign. Kin in levels above ego's in the direct line are his or her **ascendants**; kin in levels below are his or her **descendants**.

Within any genealogical level, one can distinguish **lineal kin**, that is, kin linked to ego in a direct line of descent, from **collateral kin**, that is, kin linked to ego by further steps which go at least partly in a lateral direction on the conventional diagram. Thus FF counts as lineal kin, but FFB, FFBS, and so on count as collateral kin. In ego's own level, his or her **siblings**, being children of his or her own parents, are normally counted as lineal kin. Cousins are collateral kin, by virtue of being traced through a sibling tie in some previous generation. From the point of view of any ego, his or her siblings start off new collateral lines with their own children; exactly how, of course, depends on the descent mode. It is in this way that descent groups create new branches or segments (*see* Fig. 2.1). Collateral kin of the −1 level (our nephews and nieces) are occasionally given the general and sex-neutral term **niblings**.

Siblingship is very often seen as the relationship between individuals who are the children of the same (set of) parents. This is not the only possible conception, however, and in many societies some or all of one's cousins of the same generation – especially if they are the children of one's *same-sex* siblings (that is, FBC and MZC but not MBC or FZC) – are terminologically equated with siblings and may count as siblings in a more general sense. Another possible conception is that of two unrelated same-sex individuals who have married the same person or have married into the same descent group or other unit. For example, co-wives may call each other sisters, even where no sibling tie is known. Similarly, men who stand in the relationship of WZH to each other may call each other brothers even when they are not, because they have married into the same family or descent group. The distinctions we sometimes make, of **half-siblings** (who have only one parent in common) and of **step-siblings** (the children of a subsequent spouse of ego's parent's by that spouse's previous marriage), are not always significant elsewhere, though the concept of a **uterine** brother or sister is often used for siblings who have the same mother but different fathers than ego.

Relatives related to ego by descent or filiation and not by marriage are collectively called **cognates** or **consanguines**. The latter is sometimes considered less satisfactory in that etymologically it suggests blood relationships, a notion which may not be culturally appropriate for all societies (that is, if they lack the notion of 'blood' as an image for a particular sort of relationship). Analytically opposed to cognates are **affines**, sometimes **allies**, especially in French (*alliés*), that is relatives by marriage. In some societies, however, certain individuals may have the status of both affines and consanguines to the same ego, and notions of affinity are not always the ones most familiar in the West (*see* further, chapters 4–8). A distinction is sometimes made between **primary affines**, that is, the cognates of one's spouse (for example, WF, HB) and the spouses of one's cognates (for example, MZH, ZSW), who are occasionally designated using the particle 'step-' (such as 'step-uncle, step-niece').

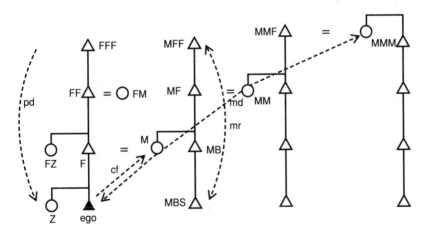

Figure 3.3 Matrilateral and matrilineal. To show the difference between ego's matrilateral relatives (mr) through complementary filiation (cf) and his matrilineal descent line (md) where patrilineal descent groups (pd) are present.

The class of cognates can be divided further, in two different ways. The first exploits the notion of lineality, isolating **agnates** or **patrilineal kin** or **patrikin**, that is, patrilineal cognates, from matrilineal cognates, that is, **matrilineal kin** or **matrikin** or **uterine kin**. The second sort of opposition distinguishes ego's **patrilateral relatives** or **patrilateral kin**, who are connected to ego through the father, from ego's **matrilateral relatives** or **matrilateral kin**, who are connected to ego through the mother (one sometimes finds **paternal**, **maternal relatives/kin** in this second sense). Laterality should not be confused with lineality, the former being an ego-oriented concept, the latter a descent-oriented concept. For example, in a society with patrilineal descent groups, the members of the natal descent group of ego's mother, although patrilineally related to each other, are ego's matri*lateral* relatives, via complementary filiation. Ego's matri*lineal* relatives would form a different group and may or may not be recognized in addition (*see* Fig. 3.3). Similarly, FM is one of ego's patrilateral relatives, but not an agnate even where descent is patrilineal, because she belongs by birth to a different line of descent from ego's FF (who *is* an agnate).

The above terms label analytical concepts and are used by the anthropologist in describing a particular kinship system, but this does not mean that equivalents are completely lacking in indigenous classifications. A society may sometimes identify and label these concepts according to its own view of things, for example the whole class of affines, or of agnates, or of matrilateral kin. Such global terms should be distinguished from kin terms in the narrow sense (*see* chapter 5): for example, in addition to specific kin terms for F, FF, FBS and so on, a society may have its own global term for the whole class of agnates into which they fall. The existence of such terms is some guarantee that the concept concerned really is a part of the indigenous view and not merely a construct of the anthropologist.

4
Marriage and Sexual Relations

Incest

Incest prohibitions or **incest taboos** prohibit ego from sexual relations with particular relatives. They appear to be present in some form universally, though their exact range varies considerably from society to society. In some societies, they may apply to little more than the nuclear family, while in others, they may cover the whole of one's descent group. In the latter case, the seriousness of the offence often diminishes with genealogical distance. The phrase **negative marriage rules** refers strictly to rules prohibiting *marriage* with particular kin types; and although in many societies they are congruent with incest prohibitions, this is not always the case.

There is also a tendency to regard incest rules as the corollary of exogamy, but the two do not match entirely: for example, a male ego is almost invariably prohibited from sexual relations with his mother, even when, as where exogamous patrilineal descent groups are present, she is born into a different descent group from his own. Moreover, unlike incest rules, not all societies have exogamous descent groups or other units but calculate the extent of sexual and marital prohibitions according to **degrees of relationship** (for example, prohibiting kin up to second or third cousin) or by specifying particular genealogical positions (incest prohibitions in respect of particular relatives certainly occur in societies with endogamous groupings too). Generally, one can say that incest rules are egocentric and govern sexual relations, while exogamy and endogamy govern marriage in relation to social groups, however defined (that is, not only descent groups; *see* below and chapter 2).

The reasons for incest prohibitions have always been a controversial matter. Naturalistic and psychological theories suffer from the wide variation in the range of prohibitions that different societies impose. Arguments that seek its cause in the familiarity engendered by the fact of siblings being brought up and living together, or the subliminal recognition that in-breeding produces harmful genetic effects, are especially problematic. The latter notion can be seen as an academic version of what is perhaps the most common folk explanation for incest prohibitions. It depends on attributing to informants a degree of exact scientific knowledge they can hardly be expected to have. Indeed, scientific thought on the matter is actually quite different, tending towards the view that even the possibility of genetic damage only arises in certain circumstances. Moreover, attitudes to incest differ considerably in intensity. Many societies view it as absurd rather than evil, because they cannot easily conceive of such a thing happening. Others may regard adultery as more serious, or at any rate more likely.

Owing to the secrecy that normally surrounds incest and the incredulity with which reports of it are often greeted, it is very difficult to estimate its frequency. Generally, it is also difficult for the *social* anthropologist to say that incest is wrong in any sense other than the fact that societies themselves usually condemn it. Such condemnation is contingent on the exact definition, if any, a particular society chooses to give it. Certainly one detrimental aspect of incest is usually reckoned to be the confusion of roles it entails, especially within the family. Of course, the family is also a locus of unequal power relations. This may play a part in cases of father-daughter incest, in which incest might also entail child sexual abuse. Yet there is still a distinction. Incest may involve individuals who are regarded as sexually mature by the society concerned but who stand in the wrong kinship category to one another. Both parties may have entered their liaison willingly; conversely, they may be ignorant of its implications, if, for example, they both belong to a formally exogamous group in which, because of its size, not all genealogical connections are exactly known. The sexual abuse of children, however, rules out the condition of sexual maturity for one party by definition and need not involve any relationship of kinship, though if it does, expected roles are again negated. Its categorization with rape reflects the violence and/or intimidation that may be involved, as well as the universal condemnation it attracts, its few defenders being unambiguously classed as deviants by the rest of society.

Perhaps the most fruitful thesis concerning the prohibition of incest has been that it is the product of exchange relations between groups. According to this view, it is the exchange of women that draws groups together to form a society. Even this view has its problems, because groups do not always exchange women on a regular basis, or at all: some may prefer to retain them (*see* further, chapter 9). An older view was that the exchange of women enabled groups to survive, because it arose as an alternative to warfare, which threatened them all. This is now generally discounted, especially since there are many societies in which regular marital exchanges and feuding go hand in hand. As with all theories that society arose out of a peace agreement between previously autonomous and antagonistic individuals or groups, this view depends on the assumption that humans once existed without society. It is actually much more likely that some form of society evolved together with humanity, given especially that our closest primate relatives are also socially organized.

Marriage

It has been found extremely difficult to define **marriage** in a universally appropriate manner. In the great majority of societies, however, it can be regarded as involving some cultural restriction on human sexual relations, perhaps restricting access for each individual to a limited number of other individuals – not always just one – or some cultural direction of such access towards specific individuals (*see* below and Chapters 5–9). On the other hand, pre- and extra-marital affairs need not be regarded as wrong and may be widely tolerated. Marriages do not invariably take place between those we would regard as persons of different sex, though the gender of one of the partners may well be culturally redefined in such cases. For example, there are societies in which women may marry other women but act as pater (a male role; *see* chapter 2) to children whose genitor (that is, biological father) is a lover of the 'wife' (this is never the regular form of marriage, of course). Another example is homosexual marriage, which is now accepted as lawful in many parts of Europe and sometimes considered legitimate elsewhere too. Distinctions between the sexes may not have the same bases or even be as clear cut as they are traditionally in the West (that is, ignoring the partial and essentially modern gender modifications of transvestism and 'sex-change operations').

While marriage in some societies is little more than an institutionalized or, at any rate, recognized relationship between two individuals, in others it is the axis of an **alliance** between families, descent groups or other social groupings, even villages and so on. The notion of alliance through marriage should be distinguished from alliances of other kinds, such as political or military ones, though in high-status groups especially, marriage alliances may have such aspects too. The alliance relationships that arise between other kin types as a result of the marriage are usually characterized as ones of **affinity**. It is sometimes suggested that this term should be restricted to same-sex relationships (for example, between brothers-in-law), but this seems unnecessarily narrow. As we have already seen (previous chapter), the usual global term for relatives by marriage is **affines**, sometimes **allies**, the latter term expressing the notion of marriage as an alliance.

Marriage is frequently accompanied by prestations, that is, property transfers, there being two basic sorts. **Bridewealth** is paid for the bride by the groom and very often by his kin group also (family, lineage segment, village, and so on), this being consonant with the fact that marriage is frequently an alliance between groups and not simply a matter affecting the marriage partners and their closest kin alone. The alternative term, **brideprice**, is often considered less satisfactory, even objectionable, because it suggests that the bride is being bought and sold like a commodity. It is also less expressive of the fact that the wealth transferred is often recirculated back and through society in exchange for other wives: often, the bride's brother can only obtain a wife once she has been married and bridewealth has been obtained for her. However, this situation is found mostly in Africa, with which the term 'bridewealth' (as opposed to 'brideprice') is thus largely associated. Whatever they are called, such payments may be regarded as compensatory, or they may be explained as securing the fertility of the wife and/or the legitimacy of the children she bears. Alternatively, they may be just part of a whole series of prestations and counter-prestations flowing between the spouse-exchange groups for years or even generations.

A **dowry**, on the other hand, is usually regarded as the major prestation, one which goes from the bride's family or kin group either to that of her husband, who may or may not pay anything in return, or else to the bride and/or her husband. In many cases the bride never has rights over any dowry and it is transferred directly from father-in-law to son-in-law along with herself, but sometimes she may be able to exercise total or partial control over its ultimate disposal. In the latter case, it is often represented as a daughter receiving her inheritance at marriage rather than at the death of her parents. Dowry is sometimes referred to as **groomprice**, on the analogy of 'brideprice', but the two situations are not really mirror-images of each other. Given that in both situations marriages are typically arranged by men, at least in public, it can be seen that dowry goes in the same direction as the bride, whereas bridewealth (or brideprice) goes in the opposite direction. A dowry is frequently found in stratified societies as an incentive for a man to ally himself with a family or group in a lower stratum, and it is less likely to be recirculated directly back into society. Cases where property goes from the groom to the bride as part of the marriage settlement are sometimes termed **dower** or **indirect dowry**.

Marriage prestations are often paid over a very long period, which sometimes extends into the following generations, and they may never be paid in full. They need not consist only of tangible things but may include or consist entirely of labour. This is termed **brideservice**, which often entails uxorilocal residence, at least temporarily. In certain societies, especially, perhaps, where there is patrilineal descent, marriage involving permanent uxorilocal residence may have a low status. In others, for example, with matrilineal or cognatic descent, it may be the norm. Bridewealth and brideservice are not necessarily mutually exclusive but may coexist in the same society, though often with a difference in status. In some cases, bridewealth may be the norm, which the poor circumvent by working for their future father-in-law. In other cases, brideservice may be the norm, which the wealthy evade through direct payment in money or kind. Ritual services for one's potential or actual affines may also be an aspect of affinal exchanges, and wedding expenses may be taken into account in calculating the total amount of bridewealth, though less usually, perhaps, that of dowry.

We have already defined **exogamy** and **endogamy** as the requirement or tendency to marry respectively outside and within a particular social group, however defined (even a village community – *see* chapter 2). If there is no particular rule, the term **agamy** is sometimes used. Marriage can also affect, or be affected by, status between the spouses and sometimes their families, spouse-exchange groups, and so on. The term **hypergamy** is applied to the situation in which a man marries a woman from an affinal group of lower status; **hypogamy** (sometimes called **reversed hypergamy**) to the situation in which a man marries a woman from an affinal group of higher status (with both words, the perspective is that of the groom; on hypogamy, *see* further, chapter 7). If it is particularly desired to stress that the two spouse-exchange groups are of equal status (in the case of a stratified society, for example), the term **isogamy** may be used. From this is derived **anisogamy**, a global term for marriages involving inequalities of status between marriage partners or alliance groups, that is, hypergamy and hypogamy together, regardless of which party is superior. Status differences frequently remain the same after the marriage as they were before. Sometimes, however, marriage may remove status differences obtaining previously. Conversely, status differences may actually be determined by the marriage itself in whole or in part: for example, if two families of equal status become allied by marriage in a society where marriages are usually status-oriented, they will henceforth be of different status, if only slightly. These considerations have nothing necessarily to do with the respective statuses of men and women *per se* in the society in question.

The situation in which an individual is allowed only one marriage partner at a time is called **monogamy**. The situation in which a man may have more than one wife simultaneously is often loosely called 'polygamy' but is properly **polygyny** (**sororal polygyny** if the co-wives are sisters, however defined). **Polyandry** denotes the marriage of a woman to more than one man simultaneously (**fraternal** or **adelphic polyandry** if the co-husbands are brothers). **Polygamy** is therefore best reserved as an umbrella term for all situations of plural marriage, polygynous and polyandrous indifferently. Despite what is often thought, polygyny is not invariably a matter of prestige and therefore restricted to the important men in the society. In many societies, the barrenness of one's first wife is a far more significant reason, perhaps even the only one accepted.

The term **sororate** may be used as an equivalent to 'sororal polygyny', but it is best reserved for the marriage of a man to his wife's sister *after the death* of his wife. Similarly, a widow may marry her late husband's brother. The latter situation is commonly called **levirate** (sometimes **ghost marriage**) but strictly, this is applicable only if the children born of the second marriage are attributed to the woman's *first* husband, even though he is dead. If, on the other hand, the children are attributed to the second husband, the situation is strictly one of **widow inheritance** (that is, inheritance of the widow by her husband's brother). There may be a relative-age restriction on the choice of brother: for example, only the husband's *younger* brother may be the levir or inherit the widow.

Thus the difference between levirate or widow inheritance and sororate, on the one hand, and fraternal polyandry and sororal polygyny, on the other, is strictly that the former involve marriage to same-sex siblings consecutively or serially, the latter simultaneously. Even where one of the former group exists, however, ego may well be allowed sexual relations with wife's sister or husband's brother even while the first spouse is still alive. In such cases, the same-sex siblings may well be members of the same alliance group and be covered by the same set of marriage prestations: for example, the payment of a single brideprice by one patrilineal descent group to another may allow a woman, once acquired, to be retained after the death of her first husband, or a substitute woman to be obtained after her own death. Thus it is frequently lineage co-members of the same generation rather than genealogical siblings who are involved. Polygamy with two or more individuals who belong to different generations (for example, polygyny with a mother and her daughter), though occasionally reported, is very much more unusual.

A society may have many different forms of marriage, ranked according to the elaborateness of the wedding, the status of the bride and/or groom and/or their respective families, whether or not the wedding is one's first, and so on. With polygyny especially, the wives themselves are very often ranked. Not all sexual pairing takes place within marriage, of course. Some societies may attempt to suppress pre- and extra-marital sexual relations entirely; others may allow or ignore them; while there are some that virtually institutionalize them. **Concubinage**, for example, is normally thought of as involving a permanent or at least long-term relationship between a man and a woman who is not his wife. The arrangement often has a formal basis in terms of residence rights and rights to maintenance, but it will very likely not have the same status as a full marriage in the same society. Any children born of the relationship may be disadvantaged relatively or absolutely in comparison with the children of a full marriage when it comes to inheritance rights. The term **polykoity** is occasionally used to describe situations of plural mating without particular reference to whether those involved are married or not. By contrast, polygamy, polygyny and polyandry necessarily refer to situations of plural *marriage*.

The socially sanctioned annulment of marriage can unproblematically be referred to as **divorce**. Its significance, however, like its incidence, varies greatly from society to society. In some cases, it may not be allowed at all, or be open to only one of the two spouses (especially the husband). In others, a casualness regarding sexual relations may make it frequent, both it and marriage itself being virtually unmarked by ritual (marriage is anyway often merely the fact of a man and woman living together, an arrangement that may well be temporary). Between these two extremes, almost any variant is possible. Women are especially likely to be affected by restrictions on their remarriage after a divorce, though these may be applied to male divorcees too. The latter statement is also true of widowhood and widowerhood, which almost invariably entail a change of status anyway, even when, as is sometimes the case, they are not thought of as bringing the marriage to an end entirely (it may be thought to continue in death, for instance). Divorce may or may not require the return of the marriage payments.

Choosing a spouse

In no society is the pairing of marriage partners completely random. To the generality of incest prohibitions and negative marriage rules, one can add considerations of wealth, status, power, personality and simple opportunity as factors restricting the choice of spouse. In some societies, however, that choice is stipulated more directly. In other words, such societies have not merely negative marriage rules but **positive marriage rules** as well.

The category of preferred spouse in societies with positive marriage rules is generally identified in the first instance by a particular kin term (*see* chapter 5). This need not restrict choice unduly, because the term for the category concerned will normally be applicable to a number of different individuals, some of whom may not have traceable genealogical links to ego. Thus one can say that there is restriction as to category, but not ordinarily as to individual within that category, except that there may sometimes be subsidiary qualifications of some sort, especially a greater degree of preference for, or a ban upon, a particular genealogical relative. If a spouse is chosen who does not come from the stipulated category, the relevant kin term may nonetheless be applied to him or her retrospectively, so that all spouses are placed within it one way or another.

Where there are positive marriage rules, and ego is required to marry a person from a particular kin category, ego will already have kin terms for his or her spouse and affines. Ego inherits or, in a sense, is born into both affinal and cognatic relationships, as well as into the requirement to marry into one particular category defined by kin term. Because the requirement must be followed in principle by all individuals in the society, generation after generation, there are no affines who are not also cognates. The requirement may help structure the whole society by defining the nature of these relationships and by drawing together the spouse-exchange groups of the society – of which there may be many – through the links it creates between them. The term **marriage alliance** is sometimes applied to this phenomenon, especially with regard to its continuity over generations. The notion of **exchange** in this context is not restricted to direct exchange between just two groups but is also applied to the indirect transfer of spouses (and of the prestations made against them) between a larger number (*see* further, chapter 7).

The marriage system in a society with positive marriage rules therefore consists in the rules governing the choice and exchange of spouses, and the character of the affinal relationships that result from their continuous operation. The analytical models of such systems, and indeed very often the systems themselves, have a regularity that is not found where positive marriage rules are absent, and this opens them up to deeper analysis and to the isolation of certain common principles. It is not enough to examine the marriage rules alone, however, precisely because of their reliance on particular kinship terms for their expression. Therefore, especially in any study of a society with positive marriage rules, we should also examine the terms themselves and *their* interrelationships in some detail.

5

Kinship (Relationship) Terminology

General

A **kin term** or **kinship term** or **relationship term** designates a particular **category** of kin or relative regarded as a single semantic unit. It can be conceptualized formally as containing one or more **kin types**, though empirically it will be applied to a number of different individuals occupying different **genealogical positions**. As already indicated briefly (chapter 1), these are essentially two different analytical concepts. For example, the English *kin term* 'uncle' designates a *category* within the indigenous English kinship terminology, this category including the *kin types* FB and MB, and very often FZH and MZH too. These kin types represent the genealogical specifications that emerge when the meaning of the indigenous term (here, 'uncle') is analysed, but in themselves they do not necessarily constitute positions on a true genealogy: a given real ego may, for example, have more than one FB but no MZH whom he or she calls 'uncle'. Only if ego had one and only one each of FB, MB, FZH and MZH would the two configurations – analytical kin types and real genealogy – actually coincide.

The whole ensemble of kinship terms is referred to as a **kinship terminology** or **relationship terminology**. The common treatment in anthropology of kin terms as genealogical denotations only may or may not reflect what is in the minds of the people being studied. Moreover, in normal usage, as well as for some, but by no means all, anthropologists, the English word 'kin' tends to suggest consanguines only and to exclude affines. This has led to a preference in some quarters for 'relationship term' rather than 'kin term' or 'kinship term', and for 'relationship terminology' rather than 'kinship terminology'. However, 'relationship term' and 'relationship terminology' are themselves open to the objection that not all relationships (patron-client, master-servant, ruler-subject, friend-friend) have anything to do with kinship. 'Kinship term' and 'kinship terminology' will accordingly be preferred in the rest of this book, with the proviso that terms for affines are understood also to be involved where appropriate.

Kinship terminologies have discernible patterns, but these vary from society to society and are not always internally consistent in the logical sense. The terminology of direct **address** often differs in detail from the terminology of **reference** used in the same society, usually consisting of fewer terms, each covering a larger number of kin types. The reference terminology represents what might be described as the 'true' classification, the definitions one might expect to find in a dictionary. For example, in English, cousins belonging genealogically to previous generations may be addressed by name or as 'uncle' or 'aunt' ('cousin' rarely being used in address), but they still remain cousins in what the society regards as the 'real' classification. The usual distinction between address and reference terminologies on the basis of the circumstances of their use, that is, respectively direct address and reference to third parties, is in one respect problematic, because both sorts of use are likely to be subject to some degree of contextualization, and therefore flexibility. This may be truer of address usage than reference, however. The address terminology has more relevance in respect of the ways in which people behave in face-to-face interaction, though it has to share its sphere of application with other designations such as names or titles. It is the reference terminology that is normally used in formal analysis, for which purpose it is deliberately collected as such through the direct questioning of informants – usually with the help of a genealogy – and not just picked up from observing its use in day-to-day interaction. The ways in which kin terms are actually used form an object of study quite distinct from their analysis as an abstract system of classification. The terminologies used by a female ego may also differ in detail from those used when ego is male. It is commonly the reference terminology used by a male ego alone that is collected in fieldwork, but ideally the ethnographer should collect the reference *and* address terminologies used by male and by female egos.

The linguistic character of kinship terminologies should be obvious, because they form one semantic domain among many within any language. In this sense, they can be compared to inventories of terms for such things as colours, animals, plants, and so on. Their anthropological significance has always been controversial, however, especially, perhaps, with regard to their degree of coherence with other social facts, such as descent mode, the system of attitudes (joking relationships, avoidance relationships, and so on) and the affinal alliance system. In general, one can say that, while the terminology will not conflict with such aspects, the degree of coherence is unlikely to be perfect. Nonetheless, it is likely to be better in some respects than in others. In particular, the fact that certain terminological patterns effectively express the continuous operation of positive marriage rules in an abstract sense is very widely, if not universally, recognized though, even here, the two are not invariably found together in fieldwork situations in the ways expected (*see* further below, and chapters 6, 7).

One can be more confident in dismissing any necessary connection between terminology and descent mode. A kinship terminology is, like the kindred, ego-focused (or egocentric), in contrast to descent groups, which, whatever the mode of descent, are ancestor-focused. Although some terminologies *can* be and regularly are plotted diagramatically in accordance with a particular descent mode, their character does not at all depend on the system of descent seen as a mode of affiliation or of recruitment to groups. The respective positions of the categories on the diagram may differ, but the characteristic equations and distinctions the terminology makes – that is, the internal composition of the categories and their overall interrelationships – are not normally affected by the descent mode in which the diagram appears to be set, much less by the descent mode of the particular society. Crow-Omaha terminologies are often regarded as an exception, in that they do isolate particular descent lines, though this is still basically a feature of the terminology and has no intrinsic connection with descent modes in societies with such terminologies (in truth, their status is very controversial; *see* chapter 9). A kinship terminology is therefore *not* an expression or reflection of descent, nor of a descent group, nor indeed of any other social grouping. For example, in some societies a woman calls her own son and her sister's son by the same term even when they belong to different patrilineal descent groups (as the woman and her sister themselves might well be after their respective marriages). Similarly, although with matrilineal descent, one's genealogical mother's brother would be in one's own descent group, other males that the terminology classes him with may well be in other descent groups. Nor do terminologies necessarily distinguish generations neatly from one another. Where they do, the concept of a **terminological level** may be useful as the analogue of 'genealogical level' (*see* chapter 3). Thus it is best to regard terminology initially as an aspect of semantics independent of social morphology, only later seeing what coherences might emerge in the course of analysis.

Genealogy and Category

The very embeddedness of kinship terms in language ensures that they are used individually as any other aspect of language, namely as lexical items labelling categories of knowledge. This means that their correct use is learned in infancy along with the acquisition of language, that is, as part of the general process of socialization. And, once learned, their use and the knowledge they convey arise immediately in the mind in response to the appropriate stimulus, without the need for much reflection or calculation on the part of the speaker. This is true of all humanity, and it is important because of persistent arguments in anthropology over the respective merits and significance of category (here, a semantic unit defined by a single kinship term) versus genealogy (where the focus is more on the links between kin types) in **kin reckoning**, that is, the ways in which the definitions of particular relationships are arrived at. Some anthropologists argue that genealogy is universally the pre-eminent factor, while others counter that it is mostly a Western obsession wrongly imputed to non-Western societies, in which category is more usually pre-eminent. Even the latter, however, generally assume that genealogy and category are alternatives not only epistemologically, but also in the sense that different societies make different choices between them.

This is a genuine distinction which has been badly formulated. Where immediate, single-step links are concerned (ego to P, G or C), it is logically impossible to say whether genealogy or category is at work. Beyond this narrow range, however, there is a choice. But whereas category, thanks to its linguistic nature, arises immediately in the mind, genealogy requires a step-by-step calculation – indeed, we talk of genealogical *reckoning*, but of categorical *statements*. In other words, category and genealogy constitute quite different approaches to knowledge. Kin identified by the English term 'uncle' are immediately identifiable by category, but only indirectly (that is, through stepwise calculation) by genealogical reckoning (as, for example, MB or FB). This means that although one category may unite several genealogical positions, it is still possible to distinguish them through descriptive expressions which refer to genealogy or some other form of stepwise calculation. In this way, a father's brother can be isolated out of the more general category of 'uncle', or a mother's brother's daughter out of the more general category of 'cousin'. This shows that genealogical reckoning really depends on the *breakdown* of categories (except where these consist of kin types linked to ego by single-step links, P, G or C). This is a further reason why category and genealogy must be seen not as socially contingent alternatives, but as alternative strategies that may easily coexist in the same society.

Even in the West, it is category that is operative for most individuals most of the time. Genealogy will be resorted to only if extra information is required: for example, details of exactly how, that is, through whom, alter is related to ego; delimitation of a particular alter out of a category that includes several; or the determination of a relationship that is suspected but not certain. Genealogy is not even a Western obsession, therefore, but something much more narrow – the tool of certain specialists (historians, inheritance lawyers, anthropologists) used by ordinary folk only in exceptional circumstances. (This distinction is not to be confused with that between address and reference.)

In non-Western societies, the situation may be similar, even to the extent that genealogy may be a means of calculating exact relationships for certain purposes, and elaborate genealogies may be maintained, especially by high-status groups; but in other such societies, genealogy appears to have no place at all, even as a means of giving relationships in more detail than category is able to do. Other criteria may be used instead, such as residence in a particular village, membership of a particular descent group or other category (in this sense, a totem or other label is also a category), relative age, or the role played or behaviour expected by particular referents in respect of ego. These may sometimes be used in combination: for example, women in a village defined as affinal in relation to ego's may be sorted from one another according to their estimated age relative to ego and to one another, according to whether they were born there or have married there (for which descent group membership or totem identification may be used), as well as according to how they themselves are related to kin already known to ego. Such criteria all involve forms of calculation rather than the immediate recognition of a single category, and the last case certainly involves a stepwise form of calculation. Whether it necessarily counts as genealogical reckoning as we know it in the West, however, must remain a further question to be established in the field, if only because the ideas of blood ties and even affinal ties on which our view of genealogy depends may not always be applicable elsewhere.

In any event, as with us, genealogy is emphasized, if at all, only on certain occasions – especially, perhaps, in high-status groups whose identity and position depend on deep, recorded, but often partly fabricated genealogies. But at least as frequent is the situation in which every member of a society is placed in a kinship category identifiable by kin term, and in which any genealogical knowledge there might be is severely limited, both vertically and horizontally. Alternatively, especially in societies which recognize most or all of their members as kin, there may be many genealogical paths through which ego can trace his or her links with a particular alter. In these circumstances, the ability to apply genealogical reckoning

is soon either exhausted or rendered confusing, while category –
which always involves definition – can be made to apply throughout any chosen universe of kin.

Types of Analysis

Various methods are used for examining the meaning of kin terms
and/or the pattern of whole terminologies. Some stress genealogy
at the expense of category. Other, more traditional ones stress
category, while using genealogical symbols as shorthand and being
prepared to allow particular genealogically defined kin types significance where appropriate. Yet others concentrate on general
features in arriving at the meanings of terms. There are also numerous purely mathematical methods, which will not be discussed
here. These approaches all distinguish the metaphorical uses of kin
terms (for example, 'father of the nation', 'father' as 'priest') from
their use for particular relatives, but there are 'cultural' and 'symbolic' approaches that take both uses into account and refuse to
give either priority.

   Formal semantic analysis concentrates on reducing categories
of kin to the minimal (that is, closest, or 'logically prior') genealogical formulas using a series of **rewrite rules (reduction, expansion** or **equivalence rules)** especially designed to that end. One or
other of the sets of genealogical abbreviations given in chapter 1 is
normally used, together with other symbols. Kin terms are explicitly seen as being built up from their component kin types, through
the logical extension of meaning from the 'primary' (that is, genealogically closest) kin types outwards. This approach is therefore
intimately linked with a strictly genealogical view of kin classification. As a result, it tends to disregard both the notion of category
and the notion of a terminology as a whole classification, that is, it
concentrates on the genealogical composition of each term and
does not go on to give a view of how the terms are related to one
another and form a system. It also relies on the assumption that the
nuclear family is the basic unit of all societies, because it is coordinate with the nearest genealogical kin types (P, G, C). This is not

only ethnographically dubious in itself (cf. chapter 3), it also confuses kin classification with social groups.

Formal semantic analysis relies on the assumption that actual human beings habitually think in terms of this 'extensionism' when thinking about kinship. One argument frequently used in support of this assumption is that an infant naturally learns the kinship terminology it should use by progressively extending its knowledge of kin types (and indeed actual kin) from the closest genealogical kin outwards, for example, from father to FB to father's cousins, and so on. This argument may be true in some cases, though there is no reason to think that the learning process is the same in all societies, especially since most research on this question has been carried out in the West. The real point, however, is that it is the *adult* classification that is being learnt, and that this forms part of the cultural tradition into which the infant is being socialized. It is therefore prior to his or her birth into that tradition. This is not to suggest that the individual cannot distinguish near kin from distant kin, nor identify, say, actual parents from parents' same-sex siblings where these belong to the same category. But the classification proper invariably takes the form of a set of categories, not a set of genealogical positions, nor a set of kin types. This is not to say that ego is bound by the classification. Although he or she certainly has to be socialized into it, genealogy or some similar stepwise way of calculating relationships is always available for delineating kin more exactly when necessary.

Because the emphasis of this method on genealogy is simultaneously an emphasis on consanguinity, the possible importance of affinal terms and kin types in terminological analysis is also neglected. This is consistent with the failure to take the whole terminology into account. In fact, not only will affines have some place in virtually any classification of kin, affinal connections are just as subject to genealogical treatment as consanguineal ones, and are very likely to feature on actual genealogies: the only difference is that the links connecting affines with one another will have different symbols (*see* above, chapter 1).

An alternative formal approach, called **componential analysis**, examines kin terms in respect not of the component kin types of each individual term, but of more general features such as gender, relative age, generation, line or side (such as patrilateral or matrilateral), consanguineal versus affinal status and so on, whether of ego, alter or some link relative. Normally, the standard genealogical formulas given in chapter 1 are avoided in favour of a special notation (there are at least two main versions, which will not be given here). Indeed, one justification given for this approach is that, although formal, it avoids bringing a specifically genealogical bias to the data. Again, however, there is a tendency to reduce terms to one basic formula, and to disregard both the idea of the terminology as a whole system and, sometimes, the possible significance of affinal kin types. Accounts of kin terms that refer to general features do not have to be formal but may consist merely of a descriptive phrase, sometimes referring to descent groups, villages, and so on, as well as the features listed above: for example, a term might be defined as 'all the males of the parents' generation in one's mother's patrilineal descent group' rather than as '(classificatory) mother's brother' (the concept 'classificatory' is discussed below). One stage closer to ethnographic specificity are the cultural and symbolic approaches briefly mentioned above which, among other things, tend not to separate out kinship terminology from other aspects of 'culture'.

Detractors of formal and componential forms of analysis frequently complain that neither of them can ever represent anything more than an objectification of the data for purposes of comparison and standardization, and that the indigenous view of the kinship system is regularly sacrificed for the sake of greater analytic comparability. The reality is a little more complicated. Although formal and componential analyses are methodologically distinct, they both claim predictability, in the sense that they give the reader the criteria for deciding which term a speaker of the language should use for any particular relative. In practice, this means cases in which a relationship is being calculated for some specific purpose, whether genealogically (in the case of formal analysis) or with reference to general features (componential analysis). The probability that a user of the terminology will ordinarily already know most relationships he or she has to deal with, and therefore both the correct category and the correct term, is disregarded. By contrast, purely descriptive and cultural or symbolic accounts all put the emphasis on ethnographic accuracy but, in doing so, make cross-cultural comparison more difficult. In other words, the breadth of comparison quickly comes to entail shallowness, while the depth of ethnographic analysis brings with it a certain narrowness.

More traditional approaches, which use genealogical notation as an analytical device rather than as an end in itself, yet are sensitive to all ethnographic realities, have certain advantages over these other approaches. They are flexible enough to be used either to describe a particular ethnographic case or to attempt cross-cultural comparisons, and they are also more suitable in examining the question of historical changes in terminological patterns. Their main advantage is that they do not commit themselves in advance, as a matter of principle, to disregarding any aspect that might be significant, whether category or genealogy, consanguinity or affinity, kin terms in isolation or the classification as a whole. In short, they strike a balance between the two extremes, which in the long run they have tended to survive. Because they lack a name, they are best considered as simply part of the anthropological mainstream.

Despite the drawbacks of those approaches that rely on genealogy, kinship terminologies are often represented by a genealogical type of diagram. They should then be distinguished rigorously from diagrams of the system of marriage exchanges or of affinal alliances, as well as from any theoretical model that can be abstracted from it. Because there is some danger of confusing alliance or marriage system with terminology where the two are represented by the same sort of diagram, and also because of the difficulties in seeing a terminology as a matter of genealogical links, it has often been felt better to represent the pattern of kinship terminologies with a matrix or box diagram (Figs. 6.1, 6.2, and 7.1 contain examples, though they represent not actual terminologies but analytical models of typical ones). This applies especially when societies with positive marriage rules are being discussed, because a genealogical form of representation tends to concentrate attention on consanguineal links at the expense of the affinal ones that are also so important in such societies.

However, the frequently encountered notion that a box diagram somehow more accurately conveys the structure of a terminology than a genealogical diagram is debatable. Despite the absence of genealogical symbols, a box diagram normally shows just the genealogical minimum specifications and can easily be read as a genealogical diagram, just as genealogical symbols on a diagram which is not intended to represent a true genealogy may stand for a single multi-member category of kin. This again emphasizes the extent to which diagrams have to be interpreted correctly and not just looked at. Probably the greatest advantage of the box diagram for kinship terminologies lies not in these theoretical considerations, but in the simple fact that it *is* a separate, non-genealogical type of diagram, thus reducing the possibility of confusion with the other uses to which a genealogical diagram might be put (*see* chapter 1).

Prescription

As already suggested (chapter 4), some terminological patterns have a particular importance in the study of societies with positive marriage rules, especially because the category designated as spouse by such rules is itself identified by kin term. In other words, certain terminological patterns are intimately related *logically* with social structures that assume the continuous operation of positive marriage rules and the alliance patterns they govern. Such patterns are sometimes called **prescriptive** because of this association with marriages the direction of which is 'prescribed' by means of the designated kin term. A prescriptive terminology expresses the alliance relationship as continuing between generations. Although actual alliances may not always have such a pattern, the inference can often be drawn that all the individuals in the society are in some way related to one another consanguineally, including affines; in other words, there are no affines who are not also consanguines (or cognates). For example, if the affinal alliance system stipulates someone defined as MBD as the marriage partner for a male ego, then MB will logically have the same term as WF, even though ego may have more than one MB but only one WF. This is therefore a terminological, rather than necessarily an actual, identity (such equations are explained in more detail in chapters 6–8). Certainly, regular cognate-affine equations are generally considered characteristic of, even as essential to, a prescriptive terminology. This is an analytical concept but not always an indigenous one; in other words, whether the kin types designated by the terms that make such equations are indigenously regarded as consanguines or as affines, or whether the distinction is made at all, cannot be predicted and differs from society to society.

The logical connection mentioned above between terminology and positive marriage rule is very often found in actual societies, but not invariably: there are equally societies with positive marriage rules but no prescriptive terminology, or vice versa, or a prescriptive terminology of a different pattern from that which the marriage rule would lead one to expect (*see* further, chapters 6 and 7). In the case of prescriptive systems, the distinction between rule and terminology is essentially that the rule *enjoins* or *regulates* a certain item of behaviour but can be broken or evaded. A kinship term, on the other hand, *defines* a particular kinship category and therefore cannot – indeed, it helps structure its user's thoughts regarding the status or quality of the category. Marriage **rules** are explicit, and certainly they become so by being expressed through language; included with them should be **preferences**, which have less the character of a regulation, breaches of which must be made good. The terminology is itself a part of the language, however, and much more intimately so: unlike a rule or preference, it cannot be disobeyed, only mistaken. Its use is socially conditioned but virtually automatic, 'taken for granted', its meaning existing, like language generally, at an altogether less conscious and explicit level. Thus it is frequently argued that the term 'prescriptive', though literally suggesting rules, is best reserved as a characterization of particular kinship terminologies, namely those that can logically be seen as the linguistic expression of positive marriage rules. This accords better with the definitional properties of terminologies, which are less evadable when compared with the stipulations produced by a rule. In a society with positive marriage rules, therefore, the rules and preferences can be seen as an expression of how the society should ideally operate, while the terminology defines the kin categories into which the society is divided and which guide spouse selection in the first instance.

The words 'in the first instance' are included to take account of the fact that the rule or preference may make further distinctions not given by the terminology (for example, identifying particular genealogical referents within the prescribed category as preferred marriage partner), though they will not normally contradict the limits set by the terminology or violate its structure. Behaviour might do so, in the sense that particular marriages might ignore the prescriptive category and take place between categories of kin whom the rules and preferences disallow or frown upon as marriage partners (this may or may not be regarded as involving incest). Naturally, the society concerned may absolutely disallow such marriages, and compel the dissolution of any that have been found to occur. But even if they are allowed to stand, a prescriptive terminology will normally reclassify the individuals involved as if the marriage had been terminologically correct. Because of this readjustment, there can ultimately be no marriage against the terminology, which, for the society concerned, is an absolute and invariable structure unaffected as such by particular, contingent events. Marriages can only violate rules or preferences, of which their relative strength is reflected in the extent to which they are obeyed: in other words, by the extent to which behaviour follows them.

Viewed simply as systems of kin classification, prescriptive terminologies can be identified by the distinctive sorts of equations and distinctions that they make, there being two basic patterns, symmetric and asymmetric (*see* below, and chapters 6, 7). In the present context, terminologies that lack such patterns can be lumped together as **non-prescriptive**, though this is essentially a negatively defined class bringing together an assortment of possible patterns that have little else in common. Another way of comparing these two basic ideas, of prescription and its absence, is with reference to the changes in classificatory use brought about by marriage. Because a society with a prescriptive terminology requires ego to marry someone for whom he or she already has a kin term, there is no necessity for that term to change, providing the marriage conforms to the rule (in practice, there may nonetheless be indi-

vidual terms for spouses). In the case of a non-prescriptive terminology, the marriage will create a new relationship for which new
terms are required (e.g. 'husband' and 'wife' in English).

Cross and Parallel: Classificatory and Descriptive

One vital analytical principle in the study of societies with positive
marriage rules, though it is also found in societies without them, is
the distinction of certain collateral kin types according to whether
their links with ego are traceable through same-sex or opposite-sex
sibling links in at least the three medial terminological levels ($+1$,
0, -1). Kin traced to ego through same-sex links (sister to sister,
brother to brother) are **parallel kin**; kin traced to ego through
opposite-sex links (brother to sister, sister to brother) are **cross kin**
(*see* Fig. 5.1). In the remoter levels, the situation becomes complicated. One recourse is to distinguish kin types in these levels as
cross or parallel according to their opposite- or same-sex links with
an intervening relative of the $+1$ or -1 level. For example, in $+2$
FF or MM are sometimes described as the 'parallel' grandparents,
and all their siblings, whether os or ss to the grandparent, are
regarded as parallel kin. Conversely, MFB will then be considered
cross kin, despite the same-sex sibling link. Similarly, in -2, the
children of a same-sex child are sometimes best regarded as parallel
kin, those of an opposite-sex child as cross kin. Thus in the $+2$ and
-2 levels, it may be the nature of the vertical, not horizontal, links
that is significant. In reality, these and all remoter levels are,
analytically, difficult to reconcile consistently with the cross-
parallel dichotomy (*see* further below).

Many terminologies, including those that express positive marriage rules, regularly, but not invariably, associate same-sex sibling
pairs by means of the same term, using a separate term for their
opposite-sex or cross-sex counterparts in the same terminological
level. This means that parallel kin have the same terms as lineal kin.
Thus in the $+1$ level, one encounters the pattern F = FB $\neq$ MB for
males and M = MZ $\neq$ FZ for females: father and mother are lineal
kin, FB and MZ parallel kin, and MB and FZ cross kin. In ego's level,
first cousins traced through same-sex sibling links in the level above

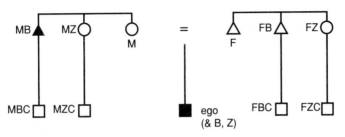

Figure 5.1 Cross cousins and parallel cousins. The outer groups (MBC, FZC) are cross cousins, the inner groups (MZC, FBC) parallel cousins.

(FBC, MZC) are **parallel cousins**, while those traced through opposite-sex links in that level (MBC, FZC) are **cross cousins**. Frequently, the former are classed terminologically with siblings – who are lineal kin in ego's level – while the latter have separate terms: thus G = PssGC ≠ PosGC. In the −1 level, one finds a more complicated pattern, because the sex of ego as well as of alter needs to be taken into account. For a male ego, the pattern is S = BS ≠ ZS for male alters and D = BD ≠ ZD for female alters. For a female ego, the pattern is S = ZS ≠ BS for male alters and D = ZD ≠ BD for female alters. Generalizing this, we arrive at the pattern C = ssGC ≠ osGC (children being lineal kin in this level). Analytically, these −1 categories can be regarded as the **reciprocals** of those in the +1 level, that is, the category in which alter places ego: here, for example, osGC is the reciprocal of PosG (MB and FZ) and ssGC of PssG (FB and MZ). This is not to say that actual terminologies necessarily consist of terms sorted neatly into **reciprocal sets**, such that each term has only one reciprocal, which mirrors all the specifications of the term exactly, no more, no less: for example, a single term for CC might have two terms as its reciprocals, PF and PM, not just one (PP).

Individual terms and terminologies that regularly associate same-sex sibling sets in this way, that is, give the same terms to same-sex collaterals as to lineal kin, are conventionally called **classificatory kinship/relationship terms** and **terminologies**. One can extend this principle of equivalence further so that, analytically, it also covers parallel cousins traced in principle through

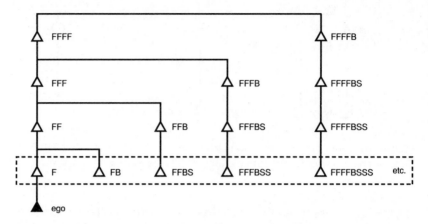

Figure 5.2 Classificatory terminological equivalence of F/FB etc. The positions within the dotted line share the same term. In principle, the line extends indefinitely to the right, covering all equivalent positions through any number of previous generations. The only qualification is that ego's father sometimes has a separate term, but the classificatory principle still applies to the remaining positions. In that case, FFBS, FFFBSS, FFFFBSSS etc. are all 'classificatory father's brothers'.

any previous generation. According to this logic, for example, a term equating F and FB would also cover FFBS [F(FBS) = F(B)], FFFBSS [F(FFBS)S = F(FB)S = FB], FFFFBSSS [F(FFFBSS)S = F(FFBS)S = F(FB)S = FB], and so on, (the symbols within rounded brackets stand for each other through the classificatory principle of equating same-sex siblings or sets of same-sex parallel cousins terminologically; *see* Fig. 5.2). In fact, the label 'classificatory' is not restricted solely to cases of equivalence between lineal and parallel kin types (such as F = FB), as the standard definition tends to suggest. Although such equations certainly count as classificatory, they do not exhaust the phenomenon: the distinction F ≠ FB may equally involve the application of the classificatory principle to the term for FB, thus covering all collateral equivalents too, so that the full pattern would logically read F ≠ FB = FFBS = FFFBSS and so on. In this example, the second and further terms of the distinction (FFBS, FFFBSS and so on) would normally be specified as 'classificatory father's brothers'. This is because it is inconvenient to have to handle such complicated sets of symbols in actual analysis, and ethnographically too their relevance is limited. Certainly, many societies use kin terms with reference to a wider number of analytical kin types than the genealogical minimum (here, FB). But where, as is often the case, genealogical knowledge is narrow, it is rarely able to accommodate such elaboration: for example, genealogical FFBS may indigenously be recognized as a type of FB, but genealogically more distant kin who are felt also to belong to that category may be included on the basis of other criteria than genealogy (membership of particular descent groups or villages, and so on; *see* above). As a result, most anthropologists – even those who emphasize category rather than genealogy in discussing terminology generally – prefer in such cases to use the minimum genealogical position, but qualified with the epithet 'classificatory' to signify that the wider analytical extensions and/or indigenous criteria for widening the minimal category are also intended.

It is thus legitimate to call any terminological equivalence between collateral alters on the basis of same-sex sibling equivalence 'classificatory'. This does not mean that the label is entirely free from objections. One is that it is ethnocentric, and that it is literally preposterous to use it to characterize a particular type of terminology. This is basically because all terminologies are in a sense classificatory, first by definition (they all classify, are all classifications), and secondly because in most if not all cases they have the characteristic of uniting at least some different kin types under single terms, although they select them differently. The English kin term *cousin*, which covers many kin types, is in the literal sense no less classificatory than a term from another language uniting F, FB, FFBS and so on in the way described above. Nonetheless, the label has survived these criticisms to become a useful way of describing the more restricted and very real terminological phenomenon of equating kin types linked through same-sex collateral links, for which sense it is best retained.

The label **descriptive**, to which 'classificatory' was originally opposed, has had an equally vexed history. One use of it is to refer to the means whereby lineal kin are regularly distinguished from parallel kin in certain terminologies. Thus a **descriptive kinship/ relationship terminology** is opposed to a classificatory one in that it distinguishes, in our example, the pattern F ≠ FB from F = FB. This particular usage of 'descriptive' is even more problematic than the label 'classificatory'. In the first place, it confuses a technique involving genealogical or stepwise reckoning with the semantic immediacy of an ordinary classification. Secondly, if descriptive kin terms can effect one distinction, they can effect any other, not just those between lineal and collateral kin. Lastly, as we have already seen, the terminological isolation of lineal from collateral kin in no way rules out the application of the classificatory principle to a number of collateral lines.

A label which expresses this difference from 'classificatory' better, because it characterizes distinctions of the type F ≠ FB more accurately, is **individualizing**. Again, the classificatory equivalence of the collateral lines is not ruled out, but one can deal, for example, with the pattern F ≠ FB = FFBS = FFFBSS and so on by saying that an individualizing term occurs for F in this otherwise classificatory scheme. The term **zero-equation** can also be used to designate a situation in which a single kin type has its own term, especially where this characterizes a terminology in whole or in part: if the term covers only one kin type, there can, by definition, be no equations with other kin types for that term.

Nowadays, by contrast, a **descriptive kinship term** is generally defined as one in which two or more indigenous terms are combined in one phrase as a circumlocution designating a particular kin type. In other words, any indigenous term that consist of a literal translation of, for example, the English phrase 'mother's brother' (there being distinct terms in this hypothetical terminology for mother and brother, but no single one for maternal uncle) can be considered a descriptive kin term. In practice, many recorded instances of such terms are probably simply descriptions of particular genealogically defined individuals who are being isolated for some temporary purpose from a wider category in the manner already discussed earlier in this chapter. There is also the problem that what appears to the anthropologist to be a descriptive term may be conceived as a single semantic unit, that is, as a normal term, by the people themselves. There are certainly terminologies that appear to have nothing but a descriptive phrase as defined above for many kin types.

In that it concentrates on same-sex or parallel links between collateral lines or between actual kin types, the classificatory concept is intimately linked with the distinction between cross and parallel (*see* above). Our initial example of a classificatory equation (F = or ≠ classificatory FB) concerned a category of kin covering kin types which were all genealogically parallel to ego. The same principle, however, can be applied analytically to ego's cross kin too. Thus the expression 'classificatory MBD' may also cover MFBSD, MMBDD, and so on. But here we begin to encounter problems in treating whole terminologies as structured through the essentially analytical and genealogically expressed distinction between cross and parallel, as defined according to the nature of the horizontal links (same sex or opposite sex) in a previous genealogical level. In the first example (classificatory FB), the horizontal links were consistently of same sex, corresponding directly to the treatment of this category as parallel kin to ego. In the case of MFBSD, we have a same-sex horizontal link in a kin type that is *cross* kin to ego, but the classificatory principle still applies, because MBD and MFBSD are parallel kin *to one another*: M(FBS)D = M(B)D. MMBDD is also cross kin to ego, but directly, because of the opposite-sex horizontal link. In the typical prescriptive terminology, she would fall into the same category as MBD – that is, MBD and MMBDD are also parallel kin to one another. Technically, this is because ego's MMBDD is MFBDD to ego's MBD: by the principle of ssG equivalence, MFBDD = MZD [M(FBD)D = M(Z)D], a parallel cousin. Alternatively, one can say that this particular terminological equivalence expresses a situation in which cross cousins intermarry, so that, for example, FBS (ego's classificatory B) marries MBD (*see* chapters 6–8). If this were the case, then MFBSD and MMBDD will fall logically into the same category, though genealogically the collateral links seem to suggest that one is parallel kin to ego and the other cross kin to ego.

There is a similar problem with the children of cross cousins where a terminology conceives of groups that are cross cousins to one another intermarrying. For example, if male ego marries his female cross cousin (PosGD), then his PosGDC will occupy the same terminological position as his own children – indeed, they will *be* his own children in the genealogically real case of such a marriage. Accordingly, they are quite likely to have the same term not only as ego's children, but also as ego's ssGC (who are his parallel kin), regardless of the opposite-sex (that is, cross) collateral link in the kin type PosGDC. This difficulty will also occur in the +2 level in such a system: MMB, a cross relative according to the nature of the horizontal link, will be terminologically equated with FF, a lineal relative, and sometimes therefore called the 'parallel' grandfather (*see* above).

Such analytical peculiarities can always be accounted for but, beyond a certain limit, they demand complicated genealogical calculations that go far beyond what is to be expected in most realistic ethnographic situations. This, together with the other problems we have mentioned, suggests that although the cross-parallel distinction is often felt to be valuable precisely because it *is* a purely analytical concept – and therefore neutral with respect to varying cultural values (including those of the West) – its usefulness is really limited to the genealogically minimal kin types to which one applies, where appropriate, the epithet 'classificatory'. Beyond this limit, the application of this distinction, as usually formulated, becomes increasingly problematic as well as, in many cases, ceasing to have much correspondence with the indigenous view of the kinship system being examined. This is the fault of indefinitely extending the genealogical approach – on which the cross-parallel distinction itself necessarily depends – in the analysis of such systems, despite the fact that actual societies do sometimes have a limited use for it in their tracing of relationships more exactly than category is normally able to do.

It will be apparent by now that there are different sorts of terminological equation and that their theoretical implications differ. Although virtually any terminology is likely to unite different genealogical positions and/or kin types under single terms, it is only with prescriptive terminologies that one also encounters the possibility that a terminological identity may actually involve the same physical individual. This is essentially because of the expectation that ego and his or her spouse and affines will already be in kin-term relationships with each other before a marriage. It is also typical of prescriptive systems that they are bounded in nature, with the result that there is often more than one genealogical path linking ego to particular alters. For instance, the equivalence MB = WF expresses the expectation that a male ego's wife will be the daughter of someone in the category that includes MB, so that this +1 male is linked to ego in two different ways. But this too needs qualifying: even if we define the kin type MB as the genealogical minimum specification (that is, mother's genealogical brother), rather than treating it as merely emblematic of a wider collection of genealogical positions, ego could very easily have more than one of them, in which case they are not all likely to be his WF too, even in a polygynous situation. Similarly, the equivalence between MB and FZH is appropriate to the expectation that mothers' brothers regularly marry fathers' sisters, as in a symmetric prescriptive system (*see* chapter 6). But again the relationship between terminology and reality is contingent, given the possibility that MB may have married not FZ but one of her classificatory equivalents (who will probably nonetheless have the same term).

The equivalence of WF and HF can normally only be terminological, because only sibling marriage could produce a situation in which they were physically identical (and they would then, of course, count rather as parents). Such marriages are not wholly unknown (at least, in historical reports; *see* chapter 9), but they hardly belong in prescriptive systems, which normally see the avoidance of siblings in marriage as essential. Different yet again are equations in which a single term unites referents of different genealogical levels, who therefore cannot be the same physical person (they may nonetheless be defined indigenously as the same individuals through, for example, reincarnation, especially if the equivalence is between alternating rather than adjacent terminological levels, for example, between FF and B). Classificatory equations of the type F = FB do not entail physical identity either.

Typologies

As one might expect, there have been a number of attempts to develop typologies for the world's kinship terminologies. Many of them are personal to particular authors, and we will discuss only the more widely used ones. The distinction between classificatory and descriptive terminologies, already discussed, was in effect the first. Dissatisfaction with it ultimately led to alternatives being suggested which, to begin with, emphasized specific patterns rather than principles of organization, as was the case with the classificatory-descriptive typology (though naturally the patterns can always be seen as the outcome of the application of particular principles). Two main typologies of this sort emerged before 1950, though neither can be considered completely satisfactory. The earlier system is perhaps to be preferred for its use of ethnographically neutral labels:

generational	F = FB = MB	(one term)
bifurcate merging	F = FB ≠ MB	(two terms)
bifurcate collateral	F ≠ FB ≠ MB	(three terms)
lineal	F ≠ FB = MB	(two terms)

For illustrative purposes, the focus here is on the +1 level of each terminological pattern, and although there is sometimes a tendency to think that the typology should be restricted to this level, it is in principle applicable to the others, for example, ego's and −1. We will use female kin types to show the patterns in these two levels:

generational	Z = PssGD = PosGD;	D = ssGD = osGD
bifurcate merging	Z = PssGD ≠ PosGD;	D = ssGD ≠ osGD
bifurcate collateral	Z ≠ PssGD ≠ PosGD;	D ≠ ssGD ≠ osGD
lineal	Z ≠ PssGD = PosGD;	D ≠ ssGD = osGD

Thus the generational and lineal patterns merge cross and parallel, patrilateral and matrilateral, but differ according to whether lineal kin are also merged or not. The two bifurcate patterns distinguish cross and parallel (and patrilateral and matrilateral in the +1 level), but differ from one another according to whether lineal kin are further distinguished from parallel kin or not.

It is sometimes tempting to regard 'bifurcate merging' as a synonym of 'classificatory', but this is misleading, because any terminology with such a pattern is likely to apply *both* terms, not just the one which merges lineal and collateral kin, to the collateral equivalents of the minimal specification: as already pointed out, the equation F = FB does not exhaust the classificatory potential of the terminological pattern F = FB ≠ MB. In practice, the bifurcate collateral and generational patterns are equally likely to entail the application of classificatory equivalence rules to some or all of the terms involved, again in respect of collaterals linked through earlier generations. The lineal pattern cannot do this, because of the conflation of the two sides and of cross and parallel. This is also a pattern that is most likely to be found in societies, like our own, with a narrow circle of recognized kin, though there are exceptions.

The two bifurcate patterns are often associated with prescription, and certainly their separation of cross and parallel, patrilateral and matrilateral, is a prerequisite for prescription. Neither sort of pattern is prescriptive as such, however, and both may be encountered with non-prescriptive terminologies (for example Crow-Omaha ones; *see* chapter 9). In this connection, the main deficiency of this typology is its disregard of certain kin types such as PGE: the pattern F = (or ≠) FB = MZH ≠ MB = FZH has very different implications from the pattern F = (or ≠) FB = MZH ≠ MB ≠ FZH, a distinction which is basically that between symmetric and asymmetric prescriptive terminologies (and is also applicable to other genealogical levels; *see* chapters 6 and 7). Although both are equally attested ethnographically, it is only the former that conventionally comes to mind when contemplating either sort of bifurcate pattern in the context of a prescriptive terminology. Moreover, no attention is given to the question of cognate-affine equations, despite their significance for prescriptive terminologies. As we have seen, the generational pattern removes all distinctions among cognates such as cross-parallel, patrilateral-matrilateral or lineal-collateral, though there are usually separate terms for affines, and there may be relative-age distinctions. This particular conflation of kin types disqualifies it as either a lineal or a prescriptive pattern, but nonetheless it is often found in one or more levels of a terminology which is otherwise prescriptive, possibly a sign of historical change in a non-prescriptive direction. (This is one fairly common example of the internal logical inconsistencies of many, if not most, actual terminologies.) The generational pattern is by no means restricted to such terminologies, however, and can be regarded as a logical and ethnographically attested terminological pattern in its own right.

The later of these two typologies concentrates on patterns in ego's level and is often described with reference to the 'cousin terminology'. Some of these patterns can be seen to correspond with the those given above:

Hawaiian	B = PssGS = PosGS
Iroquois or **Dakota**	B = PssGS ≠ PosGS
Iroquois or **Dakota**	B ≠ PssGS ≠ PosGS
Eskimo	B ≠ PssGS = PosGS
Sudanese	B ≠ FBS = or ≠ MZS ≠ MBS ≠ FZS

Thus Hawaiian corresponds to the generational pattern of the earlier typology, Eskimo to lineal, and Iroquois/Dakota to the two bifurcate patterns. Sudanese, in which each cousin (or at least each cross cousin) has a separate term as well as being distinguished from siblings, is new to this typology. **Crow** and **Omaha** (explained in chapter 9) are regularly included with it.

There are numerous problems with this typology. Although the term 'Eskimo' is normally thought to exclude classificatory (that is, lineal-parallel) equations (cf. 'lineal', above), these do occur in parts of actual Eskimo terminologies (especially in the +2 level). The two Iroquois/Dakota patterns also require discussion, for two distinct reasons. First, although there was formerly a tendency to regard the Iroquois pattern as the 'matrilineal' version of the Dakota pattern, this has little meaning in respect of kinship terminologies, upon which the influence of the mode of descent in the society is minimal, if any. (This usage has in any case largely been replaced by another, in which the label 'Iroquois' is retained but 'Dakota' dropped completely; *see* below.) Secondly, although the typology implicitly includes prescriptive terminologies with these two types, this does not in practice exhaust the sorts of terminologies they can be found with. Strictly, as with the bifurcate patterns of the earlier typology, these are a prerequisite of prescription rather than denotative of it, given again that the nature, and even the presence, of cognate-affine equations are left out of account.

An alternative usage, one which does recognize such equations, where appropriate, employs the term **Dravidian** for terminologies that are clearly prescriptive and *symmetric* in type (this is typified by the pattern B = or ≠ PssGC ≠ MBS = FZS; *see* chapter 6). This is balanced by the term **Kachin**, used for terminologies that are clearly prescriptive and *asymmetric* in type (typified by the pattern B = or ≠ PssGC ≠ MBS ≠ FZS; *see* chapter 7). Sudanese may, in some cases, represent the latter, though in others it is regarded, even by the same authors, as a pattern that accords a separate term to *each* first cousin, parallel and cross (that is, there are four terms). Because of the ambiguity surrounding the term, it is best avoided, especially for prescriptive terminologies.

More recently, the labels Iroquois and Dravidian have come to distinguish quite different sorts of terminology, this being a direct reflection of ethnographic realities. The difference relates principally to the treatment of second etc. cousins in terms of cross and parallel: first cousins and primary collaterals (that is, the nearest collateral kin to ego) are treated alike in the two cases. Basically, Dravidian terminologies characteristically exploit the principle of relative sex – the basis of the cross-parallel distinction – to the limit. Iroquois ones, on the other hand, abandon the principle as regards link relatives beyond the first. Instead, they observe the relative-sex relationship of (in the +1 level) ego's parent to alter, (in ego's level) ego's parent to alter's parent, or (in the −1 level) ego to alter's parent.

Thus in Dravidian, in the +1 level, ego's parents' same-sex cross cousins and opposite-sex parallel cousins are cross, their same-sex parallel cousins and opposite-sex cross cousins parallel. In Iroquois, all ego's parents' same-sex cousins are parallel, and all their opposite-sex ones cross. In ego's level, the treatment of first cousins is identical in the two cases. In Dravidian, however, the children of ego's parents' same-sex cross cousins and opposite-sex parallel cousins are cross (that is, MMZSC, MMBDC, FFBDC, FFZSC, MFBSC, MFZDC, FMZDC and FMBSC), those of their opposite-sex cross cousins and same-sex parallel cousins parallel (that is, MMBSC, MMZDC, FFZDC, FFBSC, MFZDC, MFBDC, FMBDC and FMZSC). In Iroquois, the children of all ego's parents' opposite-sex cousins are cross (that is, MPGSC, FPGDC), those of all their same-sex cousins parallel (that is, MPGDC, FPGSC). Thus in Dravidian, the crossness or otherwise of ego's parent's cousin and the latter's children is as important as whether that parent is of same sex or opposite sex to that cousin; in Iroquois, only the latter is significant. As for the -1 level, in Dravidian the children of one's same-sex cross cousins and opposite-sex parallel cousins are cross, those of one's same-sex parallel cousins and opposite-sex cross cousins parallel. In Iroquois, the children of one's same-sex cousins are parallel, those of one's opposite-sex cousins cross.

This is the key difference between the two types, though variants can often be identified. Another difference often claimed is that Dravidian terminologies, being prescriptive, have extensive and regular cognate-affine equations, while Iroquois ones do not. This is not diagnostic, however, especially for Iroquois, because it is not the only sort of terminology to lack such equations.

A general objection, as well as to this typology its later revisions, relates to their use of ethnographically specific labels for terminological phenomena that occur much more widely than one particular ethnic group. In general, ethnographically neutral terms are always to be preferred so as to avoid ambiguities as to their meaning (only some of which we have encountered above) and in order not to encourage inapt cross-cultural comparisons. Unfortunately, no alternative ethnographically neutral term has been advanced for some types, especially Iroquois, and Crow-Omaha (q.v. chapter 9).

More recently still, a further typology has grown up which represents a return, in a somewhat different form, to the earlier emphasis on general organizing principles rather than on patterns as such, except to some extent with prescriptive terminologies, in so far as these can be regarded as ideal types. This typology also uses the term **lineal**, but in a different sense from the earlier typology. It denotes not the isolation of lineal kin from collateral, but terminologies for which **terminological lines** can be established through the application of a basically classificatory principle. What is significant here is not only the merging of lineal and parallel kin (again in any number of lines; these are **lineal equations** according to this typology), but also the distinctions between lines (**lineal distinctions**). It is really these distinctions that are important here (FB $\neq$ MB = or $\neq$ FZH), given that nothing material is changed if lineal kin (here F) have individualizing terms. That is to say, classificatory equations of the type F = FB are necessarily associated with lineal terminologies, but lineal terminologies do not necessarily have them. Such distinctions can also be seen as splitting cross from parallel and, in the +1 level and ego's level, patrilateral and matrilateral. The ability to order a terminology as if it were composed of descent lines pertains necessarily to prescriptive terminologies and to some, but by no means all, non-prescriptive ones. In particular, those terminologies conventionally but controversially known as Crow-Omaha (*see* chapter 9), which this typology does not recognize as a separate class, can be considered lineal but non-prescriptive. Thus all prescriptive terminologies are lineal, but not all lineal terminologies are prescriptive.

Unless otherwise stated, the rest of this chapter is concerned with how this typology treats prescriptive terminologies, though much of what is said applies to lineal terminologies in general. The basic argument is that equations of the type F = FB (= FFBS = FFFBSS and so on) in the +1 level, if repeated in ego's level with B = PssGS and so on, and in −1 with S = ssGS and so on, denote the lineal or vertical unity of the **line of reference** (that is, ego's line). In the case of prescriptive terminologies, this line is opposed either to the series MB = FZH > PosGS > osGS in another line (a **two-line symmetric prescriptive terminology**; *see* chapter 6 and Fig. 6.1) or to the two series MB > MBS > MBSS and FZH > FZS > ZS in two other lines (a **three-line asymmetric prescriptive terminology**; *see* chapter 7 and Fig. 7.1). In other words, taking the three medial levels of the terminology (+1/0/−1), the line of reference (ego's line) is headed by F, and the terminology is completed either by one other line headed by a male kin type who is *simultaneously* definable as MB and FZH (a two-line terminology), or by two lines headed by two *separate* male kin types definable respectively as MB and FZH (a three-line terminology). Other terminologies may be set in a greater number of lines, and additional generations can be included (*see* chapters 6 and 7).

Terminological lines are the direct outcome of a particular *distribution* of terms, and not necessarily of direct terminological *equations* between lineally linked kin types. Such equations may nonetheless be present, especially in asymmetric prescriptive terminologies, and they are by definition at least partly present in Crow-Omaha ones (*see* chapter 9). They may also occur only in

every *second* terminological level, thus equating alternating generations only (especially four-line prescriptive terminologies, *see* chapter 6). But these are ethnographically contingent matters. Formally,
it is not necessary to have one term equating, for example, MB,
MBS and MBSS: it is enough to have separate terms, each of which
isolates particular kin types in different levels in such a way that
they can be lineally linked to one another. However many lines
there are, each line in the above examples links the male kin types
– each of which has its own term – of each genealogical level
patrilineally (that is, the links involve ego only in his own line: MB,
MBS and MBSS are patrilineally linked *to one another*).

The above examples all assume a terminology consisting of
patrilines. In some cases, it may be more logical to construct a
terminology in matrilines, so that ego's line, for example, consists
of the series M > female ego + Z > Dws + ZDws. This will not
effect the internal composition of the categories, that is, the equations between different kin types that they represent, if each category is restricted to a single genealogical level. However, where
some categories link different genealogical levels, whether these are
adjacent or alternating, a particular lineal bias (patrilineal or matrilineal) that is a feature of the terminology itself may be evident.
This will help dictate the sort of lineal bias the analyst should give
the diagram. The distinction between patrilines and matrilines is
not one between linking men lineally and linking women lineally,
but of which lineal bias is appropriate. The males linked together in
the patriline in the above example (MB > MBS > MBSS) each has
sisters (M, MBD and MBSD) who are themselves linked *patrilineally*
(that is, through their lineally linked brothers). The corresponding
matrilines running from M and MB would look quite different,
namely M > Z > ZD for females and MB > B > ZS for males. Nor
does this distinction have anything to do with the possibility that
female egos may have a somewhat different terminology, nor with
the way certain terms have a **relative-sex** rather than an
absolute-sex reference (for example, terms for ssG and osG rather
than for B and Z).

Lineal equations and distinctions as just described have much in
common with the idea of classificatory equations. However, they
emphasize better the separation of cross and parallel, and of

patrilateral and matrilateral, which the classificatory idea tends to leave implicit, as does at least the first of the two earlier typologies. In the case of prescriptive terminologies, lineal equations also conventionally include equations between parallel kin types such as MZ = FBW, FB = MZH and FBC = MZC. These in themselves would be excluded from classificatory equations as defined above, though they are often classed as such in common anthropological parlance, despite their merger of patrilateral and matrilateral relatives.

As already noted, although prescriptive terminologies are necessarily lineal, lineal equations and distinctions must be distinguished from prescriptive ones: that is to say, although the lineal distinctions are a prerequisite for a prescriptive terminology, they are not enough in themselves to establish that a terminology is prescriptive, nor the nature of the prescription. For this, one needs prescriptive or cognate-affine equations, which fall into two basic groups, symmetric (*see* chapter 6 and Fig. 6.1) and asymmetric (*see* chapter 7 and Fig. 7.1). Key examples are MB = FZH = WF = HF (symmetric) and MB = WF ≠ FZH = HF (asymmetric). Thus, while lineal (or classificatory) equations, and especially distinctions, establish terminological lines through their regular separation of cross and parallel, prescriptive ones relate the lines in such a way as to express the continuous operation of positive marriage rules between them. Logically, different rules will produce different terminological systems. It cannot be emphasized enough, however, that prescriptive terminologies, like all others, are classifications. They differ from non-prescriptive terminologies in having a logical connection with positive marriage rules, but neither the nature nor the existence of such rules can simply be read off the kinship terminology: they have to be established independently.

Terminological lines do not in themselves indicate descent groups or any other mode of actually tracing descent in the society concerned, and should not be confused with either. For instance, even where patrilineal descent groups are present, not all of ego's parallel cousins are likely to belong to his own descent group, despite the terminological equivalence: mothers' sisters' sons in particular will be in different groups if a number of mothers' sisters had married into several, and given the classificatory principle, alters in many different actual descent groups may be covered by the same term.

The epistemological bases of this typology are particularly abstract, given that descent lines are constructed for the terminology which have no necessary connection with the corresponding society's actual rule of descent as a principle of affiliation or of recruitment to groups (*see* chapter 2). The typology takes further advantage of the descent metaphor in opposing lineal terminologies (as it defines them) to **cognatic** ones, namely those, like the English one, in which kin types in different genealogical levels cannot be lineally linked. This comes from the merger of patrilateral and matrilateral, and of cross and parallel (for example, F $\neq$ PB, B $\neq$ PGS, S $\neq$ GS), which lineal terminologies distinguish. Thus, cognatic terminologies actually correspond to the so-called lineal and Eskimo patterns of the earlier typologies. The term 'lineal' therefore refers to quite opposed terminological patterns, depending on the typology one uses. Needless to say, cognatic terminologies cannot be strictly correlated with cognatic descent, any more than lineal terminologies can be correlated with either mode of unilineal descent: the association in both cases is logically coherent, but ethnographically contingent.

The significance of kinship terminologies has always been a controversial matter, but one is always justified in examining the terms with which a particular society divides its own universe of kin into categories, whether as forming a system of classification or in respect of the subtleties of their actual application. Of course, many of the difficulties have been created by anthropologists themselves: the people who actually live by such terminologies encounter no real problems. This is certainly one area where the gap between the analytical ruminations of the anthropologist and the indigenous view purportedly being described is always liable to become unacceptably wide.

Most of the rest of this book is taken up with a more detailed discussion of some of these terminological patterns and their possible correlates in respect of social morphology and social practice, beginning with prescriptive systems in chapters 6 to 8, and then treating certain non-prescriptive pseudo-systems in chapter 9. In an abstract sense, such patterns are really models with an internal logic of their own which can be treated as consistent, unified wholes actuated by that logic. Their relation to reality is not quite so straightforward, however. One certainly meets with actual terminologies which more or less consistently follow one of these patterns, but others in practice represent a mixture of features which are drawn from different patterns or are internally inconsistent in some other way. The mixing is not arbitrary and often suggests historical change in a broadly predictable, though not inevitable, fashion. This does mean, however, that ethnographically it is better to isolate particular terminological principles or features than to attempt to pigeon-hole entire terminologies with reference to them. Here, as elsewhere in the study of kinship, typologizing is no substitute for accurate description using a more or less agreed, or at least understood, vocabulary.

As regards prescriptive systems in particular, the relationship between terminology and marriage rules and the reasons for the discrepancies between them have formed a large and persistent controversy right through the history of anthropology. In the following two chapters, we will deal with the two most important models of affinal alliance system associated with positive marriage rules (seen first and foremost as terminological models), both of which have earned a particular importance in the history of the subject. It is worth remembering, however, that such systems and terminologies really concern only a relatively small proportion of the world's population: most peoples of the world lack both. As a consequence, and despite many attempts, *their* kinship systems have not yielded to the same depths of analysis.

6

Symmetric Affinal Alliance

In this and the next chapter, we will discuss the two basic and most common systems of affinal alliance that are generated by the continuous operation of positive marriage rules. Even within this class, there are, at the level of greatest detail, many variations in actual alliance systems. For purposes of analysis and comparison, however, we need a narrower range of principles, and in fact, most if not all systems of repeated affinal alliance can be reduced to one of these two basic types of exchange.

The two types differ most fundamentally in the way spouses are transferred between exchange groups. In one type, the exchange is reciprocal or symmetric, that is, one group may give women to the same group it takes them from (A > < B). In the other, exchange is asymmetric, that is, women always go in one direction between exchange groups, so that the group that gives women to one's own group is different from that which takes women from it (X > A > Y). Both types have in common a basis in the operation of positive marriage rules, but it is also important to realize that, in the analytical model, these rules are treated as being observed repeatedly, generation after generation, by all members of the society. Actual alliances are not necessarily either conceived nor conducted in such a way, and they are certainly not unchangeable nor unbreakable, but they form the basis of the way many societies are structured and are the way many peoples view their own social structure. Both types also have in common the circumstance that a

set of particular terminological equations and distinctions can logically be associated with them, though the principles for each differ
in detail.

In this chapter, we will be dealing with the symmetric exchange
of spouses. The logical assumption underlying symmetric exchange
is that women are continually exchanged between two exogamous
groups. In practice, these are very often descent groups or their
segments, but exchange groups can also, for example, be villages or
households, the latter usually lacking continuity across many generations. The typical diagram labelling only the minimal genealogical specifications shows the exchange of sisters or (from the point of
view of the previous genealogical level) daughters (*see* Fig. 6.1).
From a male ego's point of view, it shows him marrying a woman
who is classed simultaneously as his MBD and FZD; from a female
ego's point of view, it shows her marrying a man who is classed
simultaneously as her MBS and FZS. In both cases, the spouse is the
bilateral cross cousin. However, while this is useful for purposes
of exposition, it should be remembered that these are likely to be
only members of a larger category of relatives identified by the
same kin term, and that any person within that category is suitable
for exchange from the system's point of view. Thus it is a question
of marriage to the *classificatory* bilateral cross cousin (*see* chapter 5),
that is, not merely the genealogical bilateral cross cousin, but also
his or her classificatory equivalents in collateral lines. There are
certainly societies in which the genealogical cross cousin is, in fact,
rarely married, even where such a marriage is regarded as ideal in
the indigenous view; and in other societies he or she may be
expressly prohibited, only classificatory equivalents being allowed.
A corollary of this is that preferences may be expressed for or
against particular relatives within the overall category of potential
spouse in respect of, for example, age or genealogical position. A
ban on marriage to the first cross cousin would be an example of
this, as would a preference for one sort of cross cousin (MBD or
FZD) over the other. Even after all these qualifications, the above
account still represents a primarily analytical view: the prescriptive
category may be defined quite differently indigenously.

The system of classification, that is, the terminological features,
that can logically be associated with this model also assumes the

continuous operation of the rule of affinal exchange. This means first of all that there is a basic terminological opposition between ego's own exogamous group, consisting of lineal and parallel kin, and the group from which ego's group takes and that to which it gives women, consisting of cross kin and affines (some cross kin are in this group by marriage rather than birth – *see* further below). It also means that there need be no separate terms for ego's spouse's kin, who typically share terms with cross kin. Ego already has a kin term for his wife and her own immediate kin, and there is, strictly, no need to duplicate them. Nonetheless, separate terms for 'wife' and 'husband' are not uncommon even here (they may be regarded as specifying 'the woman or man from the prescribed category whom I have actually married'). There may also be separate terms for other affines in practice, especially, perhaps, EP. Yet other affines, such as MZH or WZC, logically share terms with parallel kin (*see* below).

In detail, the terminological features logically associated with a symmetric pattern of spouse exchange are as follows. In ego's level the category which includes male ego's wife may also be seen as including, not only his bilateral female cross cousin (classificatory MBD/FZD), but also BW and WZ, because the category will include all the potential spouses of male ego and his brothers. His sister's (that is, female ego's) HZ will also be included here, because the latter are potentially *her* MBD/FZD. The category which includes the brothers of MBD/FZD, that is, ego's classificatory MBS/FZS, will take wives from the category that includes his sister; hence the category MBS/FZS may also be seen as including ZH, HB and WB.

Disregarding individualizing terms – such as those for wife or husband, which may or may not be present – we see that each position on the diagram thus represents at least a set of same-sex siblings and not just a single genealogical position. The position marked for a male ego therefore covers his brothers too, but in principle it will also include his male parallel cousins (classificatory and actual FBS/MZS). Thus parallel cousins take their wives from the same category as this ego. In the same way, the category that covers ego's sister will include female parallel cousins (classificatory and actual FBD/MZD). Many such terminologies therefore equate ego's same-sex siblings with his or her same-sex parallel cousins,

Parallel/lineal			Cross		
male	female		male	female	
FF FFB MMB	MM MMZ FFZ		MF MFB FMB	FM FMZ MFZ	+2
F FB MZH	FZ MBW WM HM		MB FZH WF HF	M MZ FBW	+1
ego, B PssGS WZH HZH	ego, Z PssGD WBW HBW		PosGS H, ZH WB HB	PosGD W, BW WZ HZ	0
Sms, BS DHws WZS, HZS PosGDS	Dms, BD SWws WZD, HZD PosGDD		ZS, Sws DHms WBS, HBS PosGSS	ZD, Dws SWms WBD, HBD PosGSD	−1
SSms DSws BSS ZDS	SDms DDws BSD ZDD		DSms SSws BDS ZSS	DDms SDws BDD ZSD	−2

Figure 6.1 Formal scheme of two-line symmetric alliance. There is a double marriage in each genealogical level, e.g. F with M, FZ with MB in the +1 level. The cross-parallel distinction is also that between moieties where these exist. This distinction is not diagrammed in the +1 level, and for that reason, the box containing FZ is sometimes reversed with that containing ego's mother. Although this conforms to the cross-parallel distinction of the other generations, it nullifies the distinction between marriageable and non-marriageable women that the other generations also show. Another way to view the contrast is that the arrangement shown represents the situation before ego's father and mother have married, while the opposite arrangement shows the situation subsequently. The latter is also more in line with the idea of an egocentric kinship terminology. Most anthropologists, however, prefer the diagram shown, because it groups marriageable and non-marriageable women on the same sides in each generation. The tension between these two ways of diagramming the system is a necessary result of that system's dynamics.

1	FF MM	=	FM MF	2	
3	F FZ	=	M MB	4	
1	ego Z	=	PosGD PosGS	2	
3	S D	=	ZD ZS	4	

Figure 6.1(a) Four-section system. The four sections are 1–4. Each section unites sets of alternating generations, cross or parallel. The horizontal or generation moieties therefore consist of sections 1 + 2 and 3 + 4, the vertical moieties of sections 1 + 3 and 2 + 4. Ego marries into the section which is paired with his or hers in the same horizontal moiety but is in the opposite vertical moiety. In other words, the horizontal moieties are endogamous, the vertical moieties exogamous. Ego's children will be in one of the two remaining sections, according to the gender of ego (not ego's children).

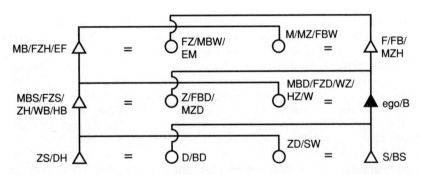

Figure 6.1(b) Genealogical model of two-line symmetric alliance (patrilines: three medial levels only).

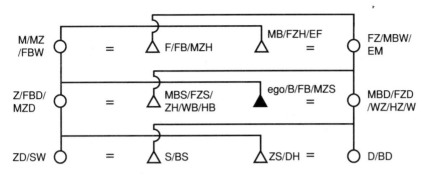

Figure 6.1(c) Genealogical model of two-line symmetric alliance (matrilines: three medial levels only).

although alternatively, there may well be separate terms (which does not conflict with the system of affinal exchange, for parallel and cross kin are still differentiated).

The basic distinction between parallel and cross relatives also occurs in +1 and −1, the two levels adjacent to ego's. The identification of cross kin with affines must be qualified a little for the +1 level. This is because FZ and MB are analytically always cross kin to ego, though in societies which have spouse-exchange groups ordered by patrilineal or matrilineal descent, they would respectively belong by birth to the same group as ego's. Conversely, either mother or father in such cases will marry into ego's group from an outside, that is, affinal group, although as ego's parents, that is, ego's +1 lineal kin, they both belong logically – and very often also terminologically – with ego's parallel kin. This expresses the fact that – assuming patrilineal descent as an example – women are not permanently attached throughout their lives to either ego's exchange group or to that of his affines, but move between them at their marriage and thus mediate between them. Here, mother and FZ are involved but, in a society with matrilineal descent, it is ego's MB and father who are the relevant categories in this sense. Because in this level too, spouses will have been exchanged between the two groups, women in the category that includes FZ will have married men in the category that includes MB: thus we obtain the equations FZ = MBW and MB = FZH. But these two categories can also be seen as containing the parents of ego's cross cousins (FZC, MBC). Because 'cross-cousin' is the category which includes ego's spouse, we can theoretically expand these equations to cover also ego's parents-in-law (ego's spouse's parents). Thus the equation FZ = MBW can be expanded into FZ = MBW = WM = HM, and the equation MB = FZH into MB = FZH = WF = HF. Similarly, FB = MZH, and MZ = FBW; and the terms for these equations may also cover father and mother respectively (parallel kin being classed with lineal kin in a thoroughly classificatory terminology).

In the −1 level, the cross-parallel distinction will also be maintained, but here we need to see matters from the points of view of male ego and female ego separately. A male ego's son will marry a woman in the category that includes ego's ZD and will hence also include his SW. His daughter will marry a man in the category that includes his ZS and will hence also include his DH. A female ego's son will marry a woman in the category that includes her BD and will hence also include her SW. Her daughter will marry a man in the category that includes her BS and will hence also include her DH. Thus we obtain the equations osGD = SW and osGS = DH, which are distinguished from daughter and son (lineal kin) respectively. Included in the same category as daughter will be ssGD; included in the same category as son will be ssGS. Spouse's siblings' children will be distinguished similarly, with WZC and HBC being included with child and ssGC, and WBC and HZC with osGC and CE.

In the +2 level, FFB, MMB, MMZ and FFZ are all analytically parallel relatives, MFB, FMB, FMZ and MFZ cross relatives (here, the distinction is governed by the nature of the ascending links, not the horizontal ones; *see* chapter 5). Of lineal kin in this level, FF and MM are logically associated with parallel kin, MF and FM with cross kin. In the −2 level, the distinction again depends on the sex of ego. Male ego's SC and female ego's DC are parallel relatives, as are BSC and ZSC, from which we obtain the global formula (G)ssCC. Male ego's DC and female ego's SC are cross relatives, as are BDC and ZSC, giving the global formula (G)osCC. The necessity for specifying the sex of ego in discussing the descending genealogical levels (−2 and −1) comes from the fact that, although children of both sexes will be born into the same exchange group, one sort (it may be either male or female) will transfer to another exchange group on marriage, and his or her lineal descendants will become cross relatives to the first group.

We will not go beyond five genealogical levels, the conventional limit in diagrams and often the limit of the terminology and of actual genealogical memory too. In the outer levels (+2, −2), even a prescriptive terminology may in practice merge all kin together, or perhaps recognize only gender distinctions. As noted already, not all the theoretically possible equations and distinctions are necessarily actually exploited by the terminology.

Designations for the particular type of symmetric affinal exchange or marriage alliance described in this chapter include:

1 **bilateral cross-cousin marriage**
2 **symmetric prescriptive alliance**
3 **Dravidian** (also used of terminologies)
4 **direct exchange**
5 **restricted exchange**

and for kinship terminology rather than for alliance as such:

6 **Iroquois** or **Dakota**
7 **bifurcate merging** or (8) **bifurcate collateral**

and

9 **two-line prescriptive** or (10) **symmetric prescriptive**

Some of these designations need further clarification (others have already been discussed in chapter 5, but they are also dealt with more briefly here for convenience). 'Prescriptive' (2) [cf. (9), (10)] is a term best reserved for kinship terminologies rather than alliance (*see* chapter 5). (3) associates the system too much with particular ethnographic areas or peoples. The 'restriction' with (5) refers to the fact that the analytical model of symmetric exchange cannot easily accommodate more than the two groups it requires (a diagram can duplicate only the structure), though in reality very many more groups may be involved (cf. 'generalized exchange', next chapter). 'Iroquois' (6) used to be synonymous with Dravidian, but nowadays it refers to a difference in the way of distributing more distant collaterals (second cousins and so on) between cross and parallel (*see* chapter 5). 'Bifurcate' (7), (8) refers to the opposition between cross and parallel, and to that between patrilateral and matrilateral. 'Two-line' (9) also refers to the distinction between cross and parallel, 'line' here being essentially a *diagrammatic* feature with which the analyst links categories in successive generations, so that one line represents 'own' kin or parallel kin and the other line represents cross kin and affines: it is therefore not synonymous with 'descent group' or 'exchange group' (*see* chapter 5).

The minimum number of alliance groups needed for symmetric affinal exchange is obviously two but, as already indicated, there may well be more, and any exchange group may be involved simultaneously in affinal exchanges with more than one other group. Sometimes there are two alliance groups that are more structured, that is, they form groups or classes with names, emblems and other attributes, each being affinal to the other. These groups are **moieties**, their relation of alliance often being called **dual organization**. In dual organization, ego's cross relatives and affines will appear in the opposite moiety to his own, which will contain only his parallel and lineal relatives (*see* Fig. 6.1). Moieties may or may not be descent-oriented; those that are may be further distinguished as **patri-** or **matrimoieties**, and may or may not be further subdivided into smaller descent groups.

In the past, the term 'moiety' was often used interchangeably with **phratry**, and the terms were even occasionally described, by different authors, as subdivisions of one another. Today, however, 'phratry' more usually suggests a somewhat looser collection of descent groups which are considered to be more closely related to one another in some way than they are to other descent groups in the society (for example, through traditions of common origins or of repeated affinal exchanges). Indeed, a tendency has grown up to emphasize division with moieties, collection with phratries. In addition, the term 'moiety' (from French *moitié*, half) can be used only if the society is divided into just two groups, whereas there can be any number of phratries. Despite the frequent association of moieties in particular with affinal alliance systems, moieties and phratries may exist for other, for example, ritual purposes, whether exclusively or in part, and neither is at all necessary to the operation of any affinal alliance system.

Sometimes there is a fourfold structure in which the society is divided vertically (into moieties as defined above) and horizontally [see Fig. 6.1(a)]. The horizontal division can be regarded as one between two sets of alternate genealogical levels ($+2/0/-2$ versus $+1/-1$), which are themselves sometimes called moieties or **generation moieties**. This may be reflected terminologically with, for example, equations between FF, B, SS, and so on. The vertical division can again be regarded as one between own group and affines, though for any ego, this is mostly significant as regards his or her own horizontal generation moiety. The resulting units are called **sections** or, in older literature, **classes** though the latter invites confusion with social stratification, which is not involved here. Typically, if male ego is in section 1, he will marry into section 2, and vice versa; his children will be in section 3 or 4, depending on what his own section is; and these two sections will intermarry, their children joining section 1 or 2 as the case may be (this is therefore not recruitment by descent in *successive* generations; cf. chapter 2). Thus, ego must marry outside his or her vertical moiety, but within his or her horizontal or generation moiety. Therefore, ego can marry into only one section, which is also that into which his or her parallel same-sex grandparent (FF or MM) married. The resulting structure is a **four-section** or, in older literature (and subject to the same sort of objection), a **four-class** system, or (less satisfactorily, because it is an ethnic name) a **Kariera** system. Attempts in the past to explain this system through the intersection of two moieties or other lines of descent, one patrilineal, the other matrilineal, eventually came to grief because it was usually necessary to recognize one of the lines as 'hidden' or 'implicit', that is, not recognized by the people themselves (cf. chapter 2).

There is an expanded version of the type of exchange described above, one which is also symmetric. This is a **four-line** system based on marriage into a category including (and minimally defined as) MMBDC/MFZDC/FMBSC/FFZSC (the bilateral *second* cross cousin, that is, the children of ego's parents' same-sex cross

1 FF =	5 FM	3 MMB =	7 MFZ	1 FFZ =	5 FMB	3 MM =	7 MF	+2
2 F =	8 M	4 MMBS/MFZS =	6 FMBD/FFZD	4 MMBD/MFZD =	6 FMBS/FFZS	2 FZ =	8 MB	+1
1 ego, B =	5 MMBDD etc.	3 MMBSS etc. =	7 MBD/FZD	1 Z =	5 MMBDS etc.	3 MMBSD etc. =	7 MBS/FZS	0
2 S =	8 MBSD/FZSD	4 MBDS/FZDS =	6 ZD	4 MBDD/FZDD =	6 ZS	2 D =	8 MBSS/FZSS	−1
1 SS =	5 ZSD	3 ZDS =	7 DD	1 SD =	5 ZSS	3 ZDD =	7 DS	−2

Figure 6.2 Four-line symmetric alliance. The numbers relate to the sections (where present) and unite sibling pairs in the same level and in every alternate level. Exchange is symmetric because each section both gives women to and takes them from its partner.

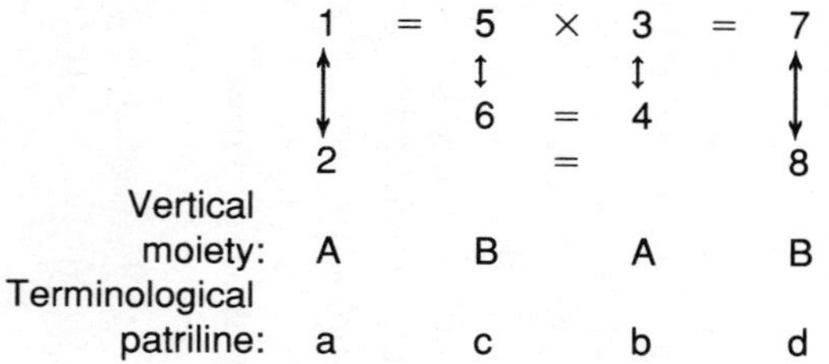

```
1  =  5  ×  3  =  7
↕         ↕
2  ←  6  =  4  →  8
```

Vertical moiety:	A	B	A	B
Terminological patriline:	a	b	c	d

Figure 6.2(a) Marriage between the sections. 1–4 form vertical moiety A, 5–8 vertical moiety B. The horizontal or generation moieties are formed of the odd- and even-numbered sections respectively. The two vertical moieties A and B each consists of two terminological patrilines and are exogamous; the horizontal moieties are endogamous. Marriages between sections and the recruitment of children to them conform to the following pattern:

1 intermarries with 5, the children are in 2 or 6
2 intermarries with 8, the children are in 1 or 7
3 intermarries with 7, the children are in 4 or 8
4 intermarries with 6, the children are in 3 or 5

cousins; *see* Fig. 6.2). In this system, the category including MBC/
FZC is the designated partner not of ego, but of the category that
includes ego's MMBSC and so on, that is, the children of ego's
parents' opposite-sex cross cousins. If there is a section system
accompanying this structure (and there need not be), it will normally be an **eight-section** system, with two sections for each
vertical line (one section in each line in each set of alternate
generations). The model typically shows ego's line allying itself
with sections in two other lines, which alternate according to the
generation. Because, however, the group allied to ego's in the
previous generation will, like ego's, be seeking a different group to
ally with in the current generation, the model requires four lines.
Less satisfactory designations for this system are **Aranda** system
(because one particular ethnic name is used for it) and **eight-class**
system (now outmoded and apt to confusion with social stratification). A variant, sometimes called the **Mara** system (after another
ethnic group), has four phratries in place of the eight sections, one
corresponding to each terminological line.

The logical connection between symmetric prescriptive terminologies and a positive marriage rule enjoining direct exchange leads
one to expect that a society that has the former will also have the
latter. This is indeed very often the case, and although, as we have
already noted, there may be genealogical or age-based restrictions
in respect of the prescribed category, in themselves they do not
normally violate the terminological prescription. One occasionally
encounters outright exceptions, however, in which there appear to
be no such rules or preferences accompanying such a terminology.
Also, a rule or preference may exist but be a contradiction of what
the terminology would logically suggest: while the terminology
may specify the classificatory bilateral cross cousin as the prescribed
spouse, there may in fact be a *unilateral* preference (for example, for
classificatory MBD), whether or not entirely banning the other
unilateral option (in this example, classificatory FZD). In some
cases, therefore, a symmetric prescriptive terminology may coexist
in practice with an essentially *asymmetric* exchange of spouses
(though this also has its own terminological consequences; *see*
chapter 7), or with no discernible preference at all.

Conversely, not all marriages by direct exchange are a matter of 'restricted exchange' viewed as a continuing system of affinal alliance. Some direct exchanges may be *ad hoc*, unrepeated and, most important of all, not expressed in the form of a positive marriage rule concerning individuals already in a categorical (kin-term) relationship with one another, that is, not between individuals already marked out as potential spouses by a particular kin term.

The two-line symmetric system that has mostly been dealt with in this chapter (defining it terminologically) is globally the most widespread of all prescriptive systems, being found in some variety or other especially in lowland South America, south and central India, parts of Indonesia and the Pacific, Australia, and parts of North America. The four-line symmetric system is best known from Australia.

7
Asymmetric Affinal Alliance

Unlike the case discussed in the previous chapter, in this system women move asymmetrically between alliance groups, so that ego's group takes women from a different group from the one it gives them to. This means that at least three groups are required, and the model usually envisages them as marrying in a circle. In comparison with symmetric exchange, we can envisage ego's group as remaining basically unchanged, while the single group consisting of cross kin is now split broadly into two separate groups, one consisting of ego's **wife-givers**, the other of ego's **wife-takers**. A male ego will take his own wife from the former but give his sister to the latter. This means that the woman he marries will be his classificatory MBD (the **matrilateral cross cousin**, that is, she is not also FZD) while, for a female ego, the correct category of spouse will be that including FZS but not including MBS. Although sometimes violated in practice, the analytical model assumes that women always flow in the same direction between any two alliance groups. Indeed, in the indigenous representation of this sort of affinal alliance system, the ban on the direct exchange of women may be more significant than any declared preference for a classificatory MBD.

Although at least three exchange groups are necessary, there may be, and frequently are, many more, which are again thought of as marrying in a circle. Reality is usually more complicated, however, for there may be many such circles, very probably intersecting with one another at certain points. In many societies with this system, most exchange groups will in practice be taking women from more than one other group. The cardinal rule, however, is that wife-takers and wife-givers should be kept conceptually distinct. Even if the direction of alliances were to be reversed, the system would be very unlikely to become a symmetric one but would simply reorient itself, thus remaining asymmetric ($X > A > Y$ would become $X < A < Y$). If this reversal were the result of a terminologically 'wrong' marriage, the individuals involved and those related to them would most likely be reclassified as if the marriage accorded with the rules. This is a possible outcome of the violation of any positive marriage rule, by virtue of the definitional properties of kinship terminologies (*see* chapter 5).

As noted already (chapter 6), an asymmetric exchange of spouses may be accompanied by a *symmetric* prescriptive kinship terminology or by a terminology that is completely non-prescriptive. Nonetheless, the system outlined above logically entails definite terminological consequences of its own which are empirically attested in many societies (though rarely with total internal logical consistency; *see* Fig. 7.1).

Let us start with the medial three levels, assuming, as is conventional, an asymmetric terminology ordered in patrilines (Figs. 7.1, 7.1(a)), and compare it with the two-line terminology described in the previous chapter (*see* Fig. 6.1). In the +1 level, the principles concerning ego's lineal and parallel kin remain the same (FB = MZH, MZ = FBW and soon), but cross kin will be sorted into wife-givers and wife-takers (in each of the sets given below, the kin types in the first equation are wife-givers and are distinguished from those in the second, who are wife-takers). In ego's level G = PssGC, as before, but cross cousins split between wife-givers and wife-takers, as do the EG and GE kin types associated with them. Thus MBD = BW = WZ ≠ FZD = HZ, and MBS = WB ≠ FZS = ZH = HB. In many actual terminologies, FZD is actually classed with sister and female parallel cousin, to emphasize that marriage with her is wrong (perhaps regarded as in some way incestuous). As for EGE kin types, these too are split: WZH and HBW (that is, EssGE), remain parallel (that is, = G, PssGC), but WBW and HZH (that is EosGE) became wife-givers' wife-givers and wife-takers' wife-

	C		A		B			d
e female / male	female	male	female	male	female	male	female	male
+2				FFZH	FFZ	FF FFB	FM FMZ MFZ	MF MFB FMB	MM MMZ	MMB
−1		FFZDS HZH	FZHZ FFZD	FZH FFZS HF	FZ HM	F FB MZH	M MZ FBW	MB WF	MBW MMBD WM	MBWB MMBS WMB
0	FZDD	FZDS DHws	FZD HZ	FZS ZH, H HB	ego, Z PssGD HBW	ego, B PssGS WZH	MBD W, BW WZ	MBS WB	MMBSD WBW	
−1	HZD	HZS	ZD Dws HBD	ZS Sws DHms HBS	Dms BD SWws WZD	Sms BS WZS	SWms MBSD WBD	MBSS WBS		
−2	DDws ZDD	DSws ZDS	DDms SDws ZSD BDD	DSms SSws ZSS BDS	SDms BSD	SSms BSS				

Figure 7.1 Asymmetric alliance. The arrow shows the direction in which women are transferred between groups. Five terminological lines are identified, the two outer ones only partially. A is ego's group, B that of his wife-givers, C that of his wife-takers; d and e are respectively wife-givers' wife-givers and wife-takers' wife-takers, equivalent respectively to ego's wife-takers and wife-givers in the minimal three-line model.

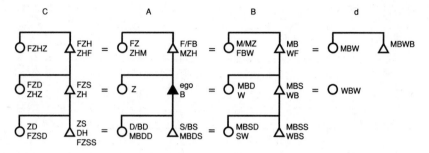

Figure 7.1(a) Genealogical model of asymmetric alliance in patrilines. In the minimal three-group model, categories under d correspond to those under C.

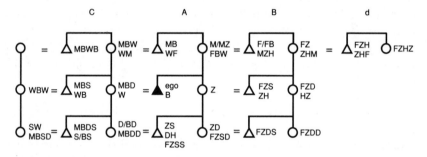

Figure 7.1(b) Genealogical model of asymmetric alliance in matrilines. In the minimal three-group model, categories under d correspond to those under C.

takers respectively (this effectively associates them with cross kin, that is, with MMBSD and FFZDS respectively). In the -1 level, one again obtains the pattern C = ssGC ≠ osGC, but EGC and CE kin types are divided so that WZC and SWws remain classified with parallel kin but HZC and DHws split off to join wife-takers' wife-takers. WBC and HBC, SWms and DHms remain cross kin but also divide, the former in each pair going with wife-givers, the latter with wife-takers. Thus as with symmetric exchange, the exact -1 level pattern takes account of the sex of ego.

In $+2$, as regards the logical properties of the model first, it is parallel kin and their siblings who are split up (compared to the model of symmetric exchange), while cross kin tend to remain more unified. Thus FF = FFB ≠ MMB (splitting ego's group from wife-givers' wife-givers), and FFZ ≠ MM = MMZ (splitting ego's group from wife-takers' wife-takers). However, MF = MFB = FMB and FM = FMZ = MFZ (as with symmetric exchange, though here these kin types are wife-givers only). In −2, similarly, SC (ms) ≠ DC (ws) (the latter are now wife-takers' wife-takers), but SC (ws) = DC (ms), as with symmetric exchange, though here these kin types are wife-takers only. Even this does not present the whole picture, because the unity of the cross categories does not apply indefinitely: for instance, FFZH, a logical member of the category MF with symmetric exchange, belongs in a separate category with asymmetric exchange. But here we reach the boundary between what one might and might not reasonably expect to find in the field. In reality, many, but by no means all, actual terminologies expressing asymmetric as well as symmetric spouse exchange settle for much simpler patterns in the two outer levels, often with just two terms distinguished as to gender in +2, and just one term for all relatives in −2.

To make the above account clearer, a terminology consisting of five patrilines was assumed, identifying not only ego's line and those of ego's wife-givers and wife-takers, but those of ego's wife-givers' wife-givers and wife-takers' wife-takers too (this is also the arrangement of Fig. 7.1). One can build a similar model with only three lines – ego's, wife-givers' and wife-takers' – which is the minimal model possible of asymmetric exchange. It is perhaps less usual ethnographically, because most asymmetric terminologies seem in practice to identify further lines, at least in part. Nonetheless, it is of interest for its own logical properties, partly because it reinforces the sense of circularity that asymmetric exchange always tends to have: wife-takers' wife-takers coincide with wife-givers, and wife-givers' wife-givers with wife-takers. Thus in ego's level, such a terminology would again split patrilateral cross cousins from matrilateral to distinguish those kin types ego may marry from those he or she may not, but it would also envisage those cross cousins who are banned to male and female egos respectively as marrying *each other* (that is, ego's MBS marries ego's FZD). For the same reason, FZD will be seen as WBW, and MBS as HZH, because female ego's HZ and male ego's WB (also FZD and MBS respectively) will also be represented as marrying each other. In −1, consequently,

HZC and WBC, FZDC and MBSC, will all fall into the same category. In +1 FZHZ = MBW, and MBWB = FZH. (In the model of a two-line symmetric terminology, FZHZ and MBWB would be equated with M and F respectively; in other words, the three-line model sees FZH and MBW as siblings to each other, whereas a two-line terminology sees them as spouses to each other.)

Models of asymmetric terminologies constructed with matrilines are certainly feasible, though ethnographically rarely, if ever, called for [*see* Fig. 7.1(b)]. Formally, however, nothing need be changed as regards the equations and distinctions characteristic of the terminology, though the attribution of terminological categories to affinal exchange groups – which is not, of course, a feature of the terminology itself – would differ considerably. Thus the category formed by MB and WF would be placed in ego's own line, like ego's M, by definition, though MB would still be cross kin to ego. F and FZ would now, therefore, be wife-takers, though still lineal kin and cross kin to ego respectively (here, of course, F is linked to ego by complementary filiation). This would shift FZH from the line of ego's wife-takers to that of ego's wife-takers' wife-takers. Conversely, ego's +1 wife-givers would now be MBW and MBWB. But by now we have entered more into the world of logical models than that of ethnographic realities. For most purposes, an understanding of asymmetric terminologies in patrilines will be sufficient.

Although the system as a whole requires at least three exchange groups, each particular exchange or marriage takes the form of a dyadic relationship, involving only two groups: the difference is that their exchanges are asymmetric (A > B, not A > < B). Thus women go in one direction, and certain classes of goods, forming bridewealth and other prestations, go in the opposite direction. This does not exclude the possibility that wife-givers may give property as well as women to their wife-takers, and ritual services may also be involved in both directions. But there will normally be some degree of asymmetry in these respects, the wife-takers usually having to part with more. These two classes of goods, distinguished according to origin, are often called 'male' (going to the wife-givers, along with the husband in a sense, and sometimes in reality, if there is uxorilocal residence) and 'female' (going to the wife-takers, along with the wife).

The asymmetry of the system usually entails a status difference between wife-givers and wife-takers, the former regularly being superior. This situation is sometimes called **hypogamy** or **reversed hypergamy** (*see* chapter 4). However, it does not normally entail the hierarchization of society as a whole. Although ego's wife-givers are superior, the circularity of the system means that, in the minimal model with three groups, ego's wife-givers' wife-givers will be the same groups as ego's wife-takers, who are inferior. This inferiority takes precedence over the theoretically double superiority of wife-givers' wife-givers. The hierarchy is therefore intransitive, that is, it obtains between any two groups, but is not transmitted through either of them to other groups. Status differences between wife-givers and wife-takers are, therefore, relative from the point of view of the society as a whole, not cumulative, as in the more familiar class or rank system, where the superior rank of A over B and of B over C necessarily entails the superiority of A over C as well (*see* Fig. 7.2). Status differences between wife-givers and wife-takers are a direct outcome of the alliance system and have no basis outside it, as with a class or caste system (the two

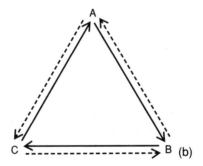

Figure 7.2 (a) Transitive status differences in a class system. If A is superior in status to B, and B to C, then A is necessarily superior to C too.

(b) Intransitive status differences with asymmetric alliance. The dotted arrows indicate increasing status, the solid arrows the movement of women. A is thus superior to B (as B's wife-givers), and B to C; but A is inferior to C, not superior, because of the circularity of the system.

sorts of hierarchy may nonetheless coexist within the same society). Indeed, the status differences that arise out of alliance tend to disappear whenever two groups in an alliance relationship suddenly cease giving spouses to each another.

This asymmetry of status may have implications for the symbolic order, and sometimes for the terminology. In the latter case, the wife-givers of ego's genealogical level may, for instance, be equated with his or her and their ascendants (including grandparents), and the wife-takers of ego's genealogical level with his or her and their descendants (including grandchildren) – that is, the terminology uses seniority and juniority to mark the status difference (*see* further, chapter 9). Sometimes this **skewing** may extend to the lines of wife-givers' wife-givers and wife-takers' wife-takers also, perhaps in such a way that they are only partially represented, that is, only ascendants of the former and descendants of the latter may actually receive terms. Symbolically, the status difference may be marked by identifying one of the two exchange groups as male, the other as female; one with right, the other with left; one with up, the other with down; one with white, the other with black; one with life, the other with death; and so on. The exact details will, of course, vary from context to context and from society to society, according to what is valued.

Designations for asymmetric affinal exchange or marriage alliance include the following:

1 **matrilateral cross-cousin marriage**
2 **asymmetric prescriptive alliance**
3 **Kachin-type marriage**
4 **indirect exchange**
5 **generalized exchange**
6 **circulating connubium**
7 **mother's brother's daughter (MBD) marriage**

and, for kinship terminology especially:

8 **three-line prescriptive**
9 **asymmetric prescriptive**

Of these, (2) uses a term ('prescriptive') which is better reserved for kinship terminology and not used for alliance [cf. (8), (9)]; (3) is too much identified with a single ethnic group; (5) refers to the fact that the cyclical model of asymmetric exchange can readily accommodate more exchange groups than the minimally required three without violence to its basic structure and without duplicating it – the circle simply has to be expanded (cf. 'restricted exchange' in chapter 6); and (6) is a term used formerly by Dutch scholars which stresses the circularity of the system ('connubium' meaning 'affinal alliance' here). The designations (1) and (7) adopt the point of view exclusively of a male ego (a female ego in this system marries a classificatory FZS or *patrilateral* cross cousin). In addition, (7) presupposes a genealogical view of what should really be regarded as a wider category than simply MBD. 'Three-line' in (8) refers to the triple distinction between ego's group, wife-givers and wife-takers in the terminology [typified by the pattern F ≠ MB ≠ FZH; *see* chapter 5, and cf. 'two-line' in chapter 6, (9)]. Designations (4) and (9) both refer to the unilateral transfer of women. As already noted, despite the expression 'three-line', kinship terminologies expressing asymmetric exchange may well identify more than three lines, though often only partially.

In asymmetric as in symmetric exchange, exchange groups may be descent groups or, more usually, segments thereof or families of some sort. They may also be defined through residence, for example, rather than through genealogy – descent groups need not even

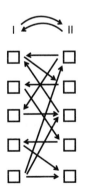

Figure 7.3 Symmetric and asymmetric alliance according to level of descent-group segmentation. I and II are the main descent groups; each box represents a segment thereof. The diagram shows asymmetric exchange between segments of I and II, but symmetric exchange between I and II as a whole.

be present. The exchange groups may not even exist for any purpose other than the exchange of women in affinal alliance.

Exchange may sometimes appear to be symmetric *and* asymmetric, according to the level of segmentation or other principle of subdivision: that is, although women may be transferred only asymmetrically between any two subunits, exchange may appear to be symmetric when viewed from the level of the more inclusive units (*see* Fig. 7.3).

The asymmetric type of alliance discussed in this chapter is associated especially with parts of Indonesia and South-east Asia, and examples are globally less widespread than the symmetric systems described in the previous chapter. Nonetheless, these two systems (two- and three-line), together with the four-line ones also considered in chapter 6, are the most numerous of those with positive marriage rules. The ethnographic existence of analytically distinct systems in more lines, and of six- and even ten- and sixteen-section systems has occasionally been postulated. The status of most of them is very uncertain, however; they are in any case rare, and they will not be dealt with here (they can all be located in the general ethnographic literature).

Two further models, again based on the notion of repeated marriage with a particular kin type, are less easy to dismiss. Because there has been considerable controversy concerning their status as identifiably distinct and feasible systems of affinal exchange, however, they are discussed separately in the next chapter.

8
FZD and ZD Marriage

While informants' statements from various parts of the world confirm the sporadic existence of preferences for FZD and ZD – classificatory or genealogical – as marriage partners, the question is, whether such preferences form the basis of distinct affinal alliance systems, or simply express variants or certain secondary aspects of the system of direct exchange discussed in chapter 6. It is especially important to distinguish model from reality in these two cases. Despite considerable controversy over the exact interpretation of the models presented in the two previous chapters (bilateral and matrilateral cross-cousin marriage), there has proved to be no particular difficulty ultimately in relating them to actual fieldwork situations. This cannot be said of the model of patrilateral cross-cousin (FZD) marriage, though it was always reasonable enough to try to conceptualize it theoretically as the logical counterpart to alliance systems based on marriage to the opposite cross cousin (that is, classificatory MBD), once these came to be recognized as both viable and as extant. Anthropologists have been less ambitious with regard to ZD marriage, which, on the whole, they have been content to leave under the overall umbrella of direct exchange through marriage with the classificatory bilateral cross cousin.

FZD Marriage

We start with the model envisaging repeated alliance through marriage to a woman classified minimally as FZD only (that is, she is not also MBD, though classificatory equivalents of FZD are also envisaged as belonging to the category), so that she marries a man she classifies as MBS only (that is, he is not also FZS, with the same proviso). This model is usually known as **father's sister's daughter (FZD) marriage** or **patrilateral cross-cousin marriage**, labels which both see the matter from the point of view of male ego only (a female ego in such a system would be marrying a *matrilateral* cross cousin). An alternative but equally unsatisfactory label, because of its use of an ethnic name, is **Trobriand-type marriage**. The system can be seen as one in which a male ego gives his sister to another man, later receiving back the daughter of this marriage for his own son. Although the model is symmetric, its reciprocity is therefore only completed in the following generation – i.e. women are exchanged, but they go in only one direction in each generation, the direction being reversed in the next. As with asymmetric affinal alliance, therefore, the model needs a minimum of three spouse-exchange groups [*see* Fig. 8.1(a)].

There has been much discussion over whether such a system does, or can, actually exist. The fact that, as a continuously functioning system, it would depend on a clear demarcation of generations would not of itself make it unviable. To work, such a demarcation would not have to be genealogical, only terminological, in such a way that the members of each generation would be seen as repeating the marriages of their classificatory parallel grandparents (FF or MM). This is also the case for the well-attested four-section symmetric system mentioned in chapter 6, though the nature of that system is in other respects different. More serious is the objection that few, if any, examples of such a system have actually been found in the field, and virtually none of the sort of terminology that would logically be associated with the analytical model. There are also doubts as to whether it would ever be distinguishable in practice from the basic system of direct exchange dealt with in chapter 6. This itself will not generally work as neatly in practice as its own analytical model suggests, because the direct and immediate reciprocity that model envisages will not be perfect, for demographic reasons. Although one can expect a general level of reciprocity over a certain period of time, there is no guarantee that there will be an equal number of marriageable women avail-

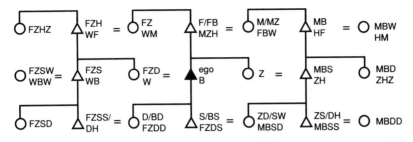

Figure 8.1 (a) Genealogical diagram of FZD marriage in patrilines. The direction of spouse exchange is reversed with every generation.

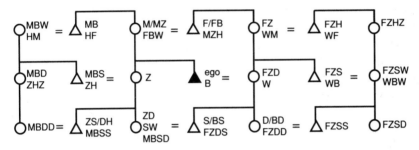

Figure 8.1(b) Genealogical diagram of FZD marriage in matrilines. The direction of spouse exchange is reversed with every generation.

able for exchange in both groups at any one moment. Thus in practice, a degree of delayed reciprocity will often be a feature of working systems of bilateral cross-cousin marriage just as much as of the analytical model of FZD marriage.

Nonetheless, informants' statements specifying a preference for a genealogical or classificatory FZD as marriage partner have been recorded in the field often enough for us to be compelled to take them seriously. The fact that it has proved difficult to match the model of a system of *continuous* affinal alliance through FZD marriage to actual field situations suggests that it should be seen as a *short-term* arrangement between particular groups or families, in which the daughter of a sister given away previously is received back as a wife for one's son. In itself, this requires only two exchange groups, not three, another circumstance linking it to the model of direct exchange through bilateral cross-cousin marriage.

In addition, the apparent lack of any specific kinship terminology expressing peated FZD marriage in the actual world suggests that declared preferences for FZD marriage simply isolate a particular referent within the wider kin category of marriageable men and women in a kinship terminology expressing *direct* exchange. Alternatively, they may simply be a way of expressing the fact that one's alliance partners owe one's own alliance group a spouse for a woman given away previously. It is also clear that such a preference can coexist with a completely non-prescriptive kinship terminology, especially, perhaps, with some variety of the Crow-Omaha ones described in chapter 9.

In reality, this whole system, and with it the idea of a continual reversal in the direction of alliance, is much more a property of the anthropologist's model than of reality. The influence of a purely genealogical point of view is readily visible in its construction. This can be shown by comparing the models of FZD marriage and MBD marriage (*see* chapter 7, and compare Fig. 7.1 with Fig. 8.1, above). The fundamental difference is that with MBD/FZS marriage, ego and alter are linked through their respective opposite-sex parents, while with FZD/MBS marriage they are linked through their respective same-sex parents. This means that, for egos of the lineally stressed sex (that is, male egos with patrilineal descent and female egos with matrilineal descent), the relevant parent with MBD/FZS marriage is an incoming spouse of the previous generation, like ego's own spouse in the present one. The spouses of the two successive generations (ego's parent and ego's cross cousin) are themselves same sex to one another and are lineally linked through the relevant PosG. Hence, there is continuity in the direction of alliance between the generations. With FZD/MBS marriage, on the other hand, the relevant parent and ego's PosG are linked to *ego* lineally and thus neither can be incoming spouses – indeed, in each case, ego's PosG marries away from the group. Moreover, ego's parent and ego's cross cousin are of opposite sex to one another and are not linked lineally. Therefore, they do not repeat each others' marriages, and there is no continuity between successive generations in the direction of spouse-transfer.

This may become clearer if we compare the two types of marriage for a male ego with patrilineally ordered exchange groups [see Fig. 8.1(a)]. This is by no means the only possible model, but it is the conventional one, something which in itself reflects a genealogical way of thinking. Male ego is a wife-taker in both cases. With MBD marriage, the key affine is ego's MB, who is also ego's father's WB, and the link woman (ego's mother) is the *spouse* of ego's father. The affinal link is therefore with someone (ego's MB) who *gave* a wife (ego's mother) to ego's group in the previous generation. In marrying his MBD, male ego is simply repeating that marriage a generation later: the women in both generations come from the same group, and therefore the direction of exchange remains the same. With FZD marriage, on the other hand, the key affine is ego's FZH, and the link woman (ego's FZ) is the *sibling* of ego's father. The affinal link is therefore with someone (ego's FZH) who *was given* a wife (ego's FZ) in the previous generation. In marrying his FZD, male ego is now, a generation later, taking a wife from that group, thus reversing the previous direction of alliance. A female ego marries FZS in the first case, who is related to her through a woman (FZ) given in marriage to the same group in the previous generation: she is therefore repeating that marriage. In the second case she marries MBS, who is related to her through a woman (her mother) who was given in marriage to her own group a generation earlier. In marrying out of the group, she is now reversing the direction of that alliance.

One can certainly produce a matrilineal account of these models, though the details would have to be altered, given that the key lineal +1 male ascendant is now MB, not father [see Fig. 8.1(b)]. The +1 affinal link would then be between MB and MBWB with MBD marriage, and between MB and father with FZD marriage. For a female ego, the links would be between MB and father with FZS marriage, and MB and MBWB with MBS marriage. The overall effect, of continuity in the former case but not in the latter, would certainly remain the same as in the patrilineal cases. In fact, however, only the latter seem to be ethnographically relevant. Indeed, as regards the matrilineal option, unambiguous examples of societies even with MBD/FZS marriage are hard enough to find, let alone ones with the far less certain FZD/MBS marriage.

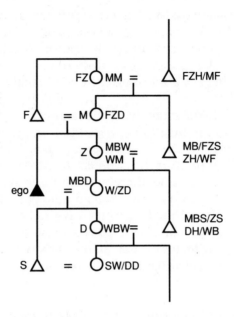

Figure 8.2 Genealogical diagram of ZD marriage in patrilines (a version in matrilines is ruled out here because genealogical ZD would be in the same line as one's mother).

ZD Marriage

Marriage between the categories minimally defined as MB and ZD can be envisaged initially as a system in which ego gives his sister to another man, and later takes a daughter born of this marriage for himself (*not* for his son, as with FZD marriage). As with bilateral exchange, the model which can be built on the basis of the continuous operation of such an arrangement shows direct exchange taking place between just two groups. The generational skewing of the diagram for ZD marriage gives it a passing resemblance to that for FZD marriage though, because the return of a woman is anticipated by a generation (ZD, not FZD), the model does not require a third group (*see* Fig. 8.2).

In fact, the terminological equations and distinctions outlined in chapter 6 for bilateral cross-cousin marriage seem in reality to govern ZD marriage also, with the caveat that a regular preference for ZD may (but need not) modify them somewhat, so that ZD is terminologically equated with the bilateral cross cousin (this may be in addition to the existence of a separate term for −1 female cross kin). Indeed, while a preference for ZD marriage may be the main one in some cases, in others it exists alongside preferences for cross cousins as partners, and any regular system of ZD marriage would logically place MBD and ZD in the same category. On this basis, however, FZD would fall into the same category as ego's mother, thus ruling FZD out as a potential marriage partner. Both equivalences are, of course, primarily terminological ones involving classificatory MBD, ZD and FZD: they do not necessarily imply any *genealogical* identity such that, for example, ego's actual MBD and actual ZD are the same person, though this may sometimes be the case. Thus further terminological modifications may occur, here and in other parts of the terminology. A restriction on ZD herself may be encountered where exogamous matrilineal descent groups are present, because genealogical ZD and MB would then belong in the same descent group. Their classificatory equivalents might not, however, and might therefore be allowed to marry. Sometimes there is also an age restriction which specifies, for example, only eZD or eZDy (MyB or MyBe for a female ego).

Designations for ZD-MB marriage include **sister's daughter's marriage** or **avuncular marriage** (after the genealogically minimal specification for the two referents principally involved, so that here at least we have labels expressing the situation from female as well as from male ego's point of view), or sometimes **oblique discontinuous exchange** (oblique, because of the generational skewing of the model; discontinuous, because direct exchange between the two exchange groups is not continuous but delayed).

Unlike FZD marriage, there have generally been less problems in accounting for ZD marriage theoretically, probably because the analytical model for it has never really acquired quite such a life of its own. Here too, such marriages are probably best regarded as a particular preference within a wider category of potential spouse that also typically includes the classificatory bilateral cross cousin. In some cases, however, it might far outweigh in importance the other possible preferences within that category. Other examples of marriage between adjacent generations (for example, FB-BD; MyZ-eZS) are occasionally reported, but they are much less likely to be the main preference in the society concerned, and they never form the basis of anything like the regular, prescriptive systems we have been discussing in this and the previous two chapters.

ZD marriage preferences are associated almost entirely with just two areas, south India and the Amazon basin of South America. FZD marriage preferences are sporadically reported from many parts of the world, including Papua New Guinea, south India and Africa. Patrilateral (FZD) and matrilateral (MBD; *see* chapter 7) cross-cousin marriages are often placed together under the umbrella term **unilateral cross-cousin marriage**, in opposition to the bilateral cross-cousin marriage or symmetric spouse exchange dealt with in chapter 6.

9
Non-prescriptive Pseudo-systems

Elementary and Complex Structures

Societies with positive marriage rules are often called **elementary structures**, because the affinal alliance systems that are based upon such rules can be modelled in terms of the continual operation of a simple ('elementary') marriage rule. Terminologically, these are, of course, prescriptive systems. They are often contrasted with **complex structures**, that is, those that cannot be conceptualized so simply, because they do not use a kin term to identify a particular category from which the spouse should be taken. Instead, other considerations come into play (wealth, status, romantic love), which cannot be reduced to a simple rule in the same way. Under such circumstances, it is difficult to see them as structures at all in the same sense, for they are really a negatively defined class. They tend to place marriage beyond the range of recognized kin, who approximate to the closer genealogical relatives. Remoter relatives may be allowed, non-relatives normally are allowed. However, the boundary between marriageable and non-marriageable kin is not at all predictable in such cases.

Crow-Omaha or Semi-complex Structures

Sometimes a class of societies is postulated as intermediate between elementary and complex structures; these are called **semi-**

complex structures or **Crow-Omaha** systems. Like complex structures, semi-complex structures are terminologically non-prescriptive. The status of the latter is a controversial matter, however, and there are different views of exactly what is involved. As with the equally controversial systems described in chapter 8, it is especially important to separate model from reality in these cases.

There are two basic approaches to defining such systems in modern anthropology: one focuses on the terminologies, the other on affinal alliance. Terminologically, Crow-Omaha systems are usually defined by the various equations they make between cross cousins and certain lineal ascendants and descendants. The labels 'Crow' and 'Omaha' are taken from the names of two North American ethnic groups in whose terminologies these types of equations were early identified. They are found more widely than in North America, however – where they are certainly not restricted to these two groups – and the designations 'Crow', 'Omaha' and 'Crow-Omaha' are therefore unhappy ones. Unfortunately, not even the expression 'semi-complex structures' is a generally accepted alternative (it does not distinguish between the two basic varieties of equation, as 'Crow-Omaha' does). Thus the older expressions will be retained here.

Crow (sometimes **Choctaw** in older texts) equations conven-

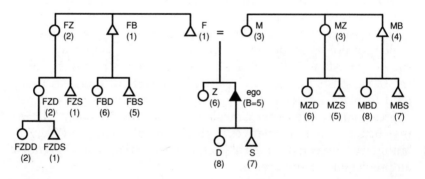

Figure 9.1 Crow terminological equivalences. Kin types with the same numbers have the same term. Term 2 traces out the matriline of ego's FZ, i.e. ego's +1 patrilateral cross kin; term 1 unites the males of that line. Terms 7 and 8 unite female ego's BC or male ego's own children with their matrilateral cross cousins.

tionally express the *matrilineal* unity of particular kin types (*see* Fig. 9.1):

F = FB = FZS (sometimes also FZDS; males of ego's father's matriline, especially ascending)

FZ = FZD (sometimes also FZDD; females of ego's father's matriline, especially ascending)

MBS = S (ms) = BS (ws)

MBD = D (ms) = BD (ws)

Omaha equations conventionally express the *patrilineal* unity of particular kin types (*see* Fig. 9.2):

MB = MBS (sometimes also MBSS; males of ego's mother's patriline, especially ascending)

M = MZ = MBD (sometimes also MBSD; females of ego's mother's patriline, especially ascending)

FZS = ZS (ms) = S (ws)

FZD = ZD (ms) = D (ws)

Thus certain interlevel equations in these models link members of the descent lines of ego's near kin, though not that of ego himself.

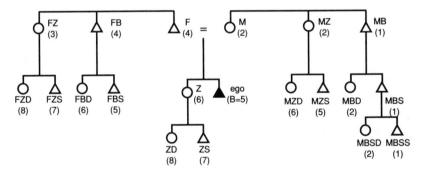

Figure 9.2 Omaha terminological equivalences. Kin types with the same numbers have the same term. Term 1 traces out the patriline of ego's MB, i.e. ego's +1 matrilateral cross kin; term 2 unites the females of that line. Terms 7 and 8 unite male ego's ZC or female ego's own children with their patrilateral cross cousins.

In particular, the equations that link ego's genealogical level with the +1 level would trace out the line linked to him through complementary filiation (*see* chapter 2) if the descent mode agreed with the terminological pattern. This means the line of the father in a society with matrilineal descent and Crow equations, and the line of the mother in a society with patrilineal descent and Omaha equations. This lineal bias, ascending on one side of the terminology and descending on the other, is sometimes called **skewing**. As models, these terminologies are thus asymmetric, but nonprescriptive (although actual prescriptive terminologies, especially asymmetric ones, sometimes have similar equations; *see* below). They can also be considered lineal in the second of the senses given in chapter 5, because of their considerable vertical unity. Indeed, those who follow the lineal-cognatic typology in respect of kinship terminologies tend not to recognize a separate class of Crow-Omaha terminologies as such, but to class those known elsewhere by the label as lineal.

The vertical unity of Crow-Omaha terminologies comes partly from the direct equations given above, and partly from classificatory equations of the type $P = PssG$ and $G = PssGC$, and the distinctions between patrilateral and matrilateral, cross and parallel, that these entail. It is the nature of the vertical equations that defines each terminological model and gives it its particular lineal bias. Any unity in the other lines comes only from the *distribution* of separate terms, as described in the second sense of lineal in chapter 5. It is only the vertical *equations* that have struck anthropologists as worthy of attention in these models, but the recognition that they also have terminological lines of a different composition is useful at least in showing further how they differ from prescriptive ones (as already stated, all prescriptive terminologies are lineal, but not all lineal terminologies are prescriptive). One difference is the usual presence of distinct lines composed solely of affines, which it is legitimate to recognize as lines so long as the categories involved can be linked by lineal descent (that is, by the hypothetical descent of a terminological line; for example, $WF > WB > WBS$). Again, the lines may consist either of a mere distribution of terms according to one of the unilineal descent modes, or of actual vertical terminological equations. Only if such kin types were systematically equated with cross kin in every generation could one talk of prescription. The lack of prescriptive equations in these terminological models means that however the different lines are constructed, they are not systematically linked in each generation by the continual operation of a positive marriage rule, as in a prescriptive system, but only initially, through the marriage of ego's parents. Usually, this is the only marriage shown in diagrams of Crow-Omaha systems: prescriptive models, by contrast, show as many marriages as opposite-sex sibling links. This can be regarded as another diagnostic difference between the two sorts of model.

There was a tendency in the past to regard the vertical terminological equations of Crow-Omaha systems simply as an expression of descent group unity. In the first place, however, this is to confuse lineal identity in a terminology – an egocentric point of view – with the existence of sociocentric descent groups. Secondly, although vertical equations may occur in other parts of a terminology than those already indicated, including occasionally ego's own line, those in the models themselves occur only in one descent line, a not very impressive display of descent-group unity. Thirdly, even this cannot explain those equations that unite one set of cross cousins with a set of -1 referents, for, with exogamous unilineal descent groups, the latter would invariably be in a different descent group. Fourthly, not all societies with Crow-Omaha terminologies have unilineal descent groups of either sort, and comparatively few societies with unilineal descent have Crow-Omaha terminologies. Fifthly, the correlations between Crow equations and matrilineal descent, on the one hand, and between Omaha equations and patrilineal descent, on the other, are no more than tendencies, though admittedly quite strong ones. Finally, such terminological features are often found piecemeal rather than as characterizing whole terminologies, to such an extent that, for some anthropologists, the equations FZ = FZD and MB = MBS are enough to define a terminology as Crow or Omaha respectively. Such a narrow definition has little value, because terminologies with such minimal equations tend to differ widely in other respects and do not form any sort of class in themselves.

As already noted, a later tendency sought an answer in the

circumstances of affinal alliance. In this view, Crow-Omaha terminologies are regularly associated with, indeed seen as, semi-complex structures, which themselves are defined by their prohibitions on the immediate repetition of marriages between particular descent groups, that is, through a sociological rather than a terminological feature. Such prohibitions are said to exploit the terminological devices listed above in that the latter equate kin types in descent groups consisting of close kin, who are themselves prohibited as marriage partners. Bans on the repetition will normally last for a restricted number of generations – even just one – as previous genealogical connections become dimly remembered or unimportant. The effect of such prohibitions is to disperse the alliances of a descent group among a number of other such groups. This in its turn makes cognate-affine equations in the terminology redundant, because affines are not also cognates by virtue of previous alliances. In other words, there is a clear logical connection between the ban on the immediate repetition of marriage between descent groups and the lack of prescriptive equations linking terminological lines systematically (*see* above).

Such societies thus lack positive marriage rules but, in prohibiting marriage with certain kin types, they refer to category or kinship term rather than to genealogical position: as a consequence, it is argued that they have something of the character of both elementary and complex structures. This interpretation, too, is only partially supported ethnographically, however. First, it is not only Crow-Omaha systems that identify relatives prohibited in marriage through kin term – indeed, this is true of any terminology, to the extent that it helps govern, along with genealogical specifications and degrees of relationship, the operation of incest rules and negative marriage rules (as well as positive marriage rules where these occur). Secondly, as already stated above and in chapter 7, some societies with positive marriage rules enjoining asymmetric affinal alliance have terminological equations linking referents of ego's level with ascendants or descendants respectively. These equations not only skew the terminology, they sometimes resemble directly the standard Crow-Omaha ones given above, which are therefore not associated solely with the *absence* of such rules. In other words,

Crow-Omaha equations often coexist with cognate-affine or pre-scriptive ones.

Thirdly, while there are certainly societies with dispersed alliance in the sense defined above, they by no means always have Crow-Omaha terminologies, nor do the latter always occur with dispersed alliance. Fourthly, the practice of dispersing alliances is not re-stricted to complex or semi-complex systems of affinal alliance, but may be a feature of societies with positive marriage rules too. Here, however, the dispersal usually concerns the marriages of a group of siblings in the same generation rather than those in successive generations (for example, only one sibling may or must obey the prescription). As a result, there may be no generational delay before the alliance can be renewed. Indeed, as we have seen, inter-generational repetition is a key feature of the model of this sort of alliance system and gives it its continuity, though it is not invariably found in practice. Lastly, these arguments regularly assume that a spouse-exchange group is necessarily a descent group, an assump-tion based on the descent lines formed by the vertical equations of the terminological model: we have seen in previous chapters that the two are not necessarily coordinate.

It is thus a controversial matter whether Crow-Omaha or semi-complex systems form an identifiable class of alliance or descent or even terminological system. Certainly, vertical terminological equations covering successive genealogical levels do exist, and equally certainly, commonly occurring features can be discerned. Similarly, there are many societies that disperse alliances among a number of alliance groups by delaying immediate repetition be-tween any two. The problem lies in assessing the extent to which these two features can regularly be associated with one another ethnographically. We have seen that this also applies to prescriptive systems, in the sense that the marriage rules and preferences of a particular society do not always correspond with what one would logically expect from the pattern of the terminology in that society. In these cases, however, there is a wider measure of agreement that prescriptive terminologies do have definite reflexes at the levels of rules and behaviour, in the sense that particular patterns of alliance exist that they more or less express. In the case of Crow-Omaha systems, there is little agreement over whether they have such reflexes at all, let alone as to what these are. In that sense, they lie at the limit of what is analytically definable and explicable.

Ultimately, the difference comes down to the closure, that is, boundedness, of prescriptive systems, which is lacking with Crow-Omaha systems. The model of symmetric spouse exchange discussed in chapter 6 has the most obvious degree of closure because it presupposes only two spouse-exchange groups (or two terminological lines). Any kin type, however long the genealogical chain used to represent it, and regardless of how many affinal ties it includes, can be traced to a position within the model. This is because the regularity of cognate-affine equations in the system creates a multiplicity of alternative genealogical paths between ego and many alters. Prescriptive systems are defined by such equations and are characterized by the constant and regular repetition of marriages between the lines. As a result, the vertical dimension will consist of a number of affinal links, interspersed with an exactly equivalent number of opposite-sex sibling links.

The fact that this model cannot be expanded to show additional lines and still retain its structure – it can only be duplicated – is a virtue in this context. The model of asymmetric spouse exchange (chapter 7) also has closure by reason of its cognate-affine equations and its circularity. The only difference is that, in this case, there is a potential difference of scale. The fact that a third line has to be introduced to accommodate the division of cross kin and affines into wife-givers and wife-takers means that the model can, in principle, be expanded indefinitely, through the addition of yet more lines. This will not in itself compromise the degree of either closure or recursiveness but, beyond a certain limit of expansion, the model becomes cognitively unmanageable. This problem can be solved by limiting it to the necessary three lines, so that ego's wife-givers take wives from ego's wife-takers.

The same sort of closure, and for the same reasons, is also found in the models of four-line symmetric systems (chapter 6) and of ZD marriage and FZD marriage (chapter 8), showing that, whatever the controversy surrounding the latter two on ethnographic grounds, as models they are prescriptive. But neither closure nor recursiveness are features of models of Crow-Omaha systems, however elaborate. Although a high number of opposite-sex sibling links will be shown, only one marriage, that of ego's parents, is necessary to show the characteristic terminological equivalences on a diagram. One result of this is to make the terminological treatment of ego's affines irrelevant (*see* Figs. 9.1 and 9.2). This also means that the multiplicity of genealogical paths between any two positions is lacking. And, because affinal connections are elaborated outside the model (as it is defined), extending themselves *ad infinitum* instead of returning recursively within it, it has no closure. The lengths of genealogical chains therefore become significant, in the sense that the longer they are, the more difficult it is for the model to accommodate them.

This very lack of closure is reason enough to doubt that a 'Crow-Omaha system' actually exists. This is not to say that societies with such features in their kinship terminologies lack kinship systems, but it does suggest that the systems cannot be defined with reference to the features.

Parallel Cousin Marriage

In some societies – mainly Islamic ones in North Africa, the Middle East and western Asia – marriages are consolidated rather than dispersed, through the device of marriage between the children of two brothers, that is, **patrilateral parallel cousin marriage** or **FBD marriage**. In this system, male ego marries FBD, while female ego marries FBS [*see* Fig. 9.3(a)]. The occasional examples of marriages between full or classificatory siblings (for example, parallel cousins) or half-siblings, reported historically for certain elite groups especially, can be grouped with them.

One basic contrast between parallel-cousin and sibling marriages, on the one hand, and cross-cousin marriages (or positive marriage rules), on the other, is often said to be the difference between isolating and integrating different groups (often but not always descent groups) in the society through marriage. In the former case, one marries within a group or class, and links to other groups or classes in the society have to be made in other ways, if at all: the notion of alliance through marriage is generally considered less appropriate. In the latter case, on the other hand, affinal alliance through marriage is a chief mechanism whereby such groups are integrated into the society. This may be thought to affect property and power also, which are supposedly retained within a narrow range of kin in the former case but dispersed among different groups in the latter. In fact, an exogamous system may circulate or accumulate wealth as well as disperse it. Both tendencies may even occur in the same society, one of a set of brothers marrying FBD, that is, endogamously, the others marrying exogamously (which will almost certainly not mean prescriptively in such cases).

In any case, there are no necessary links between endogamy, exogamy and marriage to particular kin types. Certainly where exogamous unilineal descent groups exist, both sets of cross cousins will be outside ego's group and therefore marriageable, while at least one set of parallel cousins will be within it and therefore unmarriageable. Even here, however, parallel cousins linked to ego through ties of complementary filiation (for example, MZC in a society with patrilineal descent groups) will not be in ego's group if ego's mother and MZ married into different groups. Under such circumstances, MZC marriage may be allowed though, unlike FBC marriage, it is rarely if ever considered ideal. Also, even cross-cousin marriage can quite easily coexist with endogamous institutions that are not the actual affinal alliance units (for example, endogamous cognatic descent groups or kindreds, villages, classes or castes; none of these except the last is *necessarily* endogamous). Another way of looking at FBC marriage, therefore, is simply that it results from a preference for marriage between particular close agnates, for which the concentration of power and property serves as rationalization rather than reason. In some cases, the very fact of marriage may be taken as indicating the presence of agnatic links that are otherwise undemonstrable.

Even if allowed, sibling marriages are hardly feasible as the main form of marriage in any society. On the other hand, FBD-FBS marriage sometimes appears to be quite systematic, in the sense that it is the preference most widely followed in the society. Nevertheless, it is not generally counted as constituting a positive marriage rule or the basis of a prescriptive system. One reason for this is the lack of particular terminological features expressing its con-

Figure 9.3 (a) Minimal diagram of FBC marriage. Note the imbalance in male and female symbols compared with diagrams of prescriptive systems.

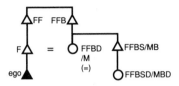

Figure 9.3 (b) FBC marriage repeated in two generations. Male ego's second patrilateral parallel cousins are also his first matrilateral cross cousins (i.e. MBC); to them, he is both second patrilateral parallel cousin and first patrilateral cross cousin (i.e. FZS).

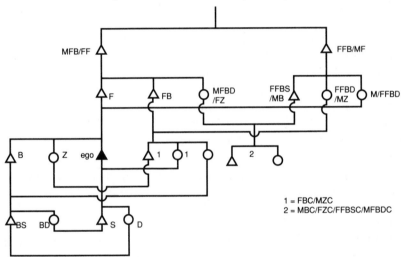

Figure 9.3 (c) Diagram of FBC marriage repeated over three generations. Even though every marriage shown has taken place between an FBS and an FBD, the lack of regularity compared with the diagram of any prescriptive system will be obvious. Some symbols are shown, quite unrealistically, as unmarried, but the structure can be completed only by introducing yet more collateral lines, by introducing symbols for parallel kin, and by duplicating symbols for certain kin types (e.g. FBD on this diagram). Thus, the diagram tends to resemble a genealogy rather than an abstract system of classification. Note that the symbols on the diagram are consanguineally linked and form one patrilineal descent group.

tinual operation, a defining feature of a prescriptive system. Moreover, cases in which the rule is not followed are less likely to entail the retrospective terminological redefinition typical of prescriptive systems. There may also be a greater tendency, compared with prescriptive systems, for genealogy or degree of relationship to be used rather than category in identifying a suitable spouse. Nonetheless, terminological equivalence between actual and classificatory FBC is common, and classificatory equivalents may be allowed or specified in preference to first parallel cousins.

In reality, the continual operation of a rule of FBC marriage often results in a confused network of cousin relationships, some of which can equally be seen as matrilateral and/or cross as patrilateral and parallel: this is another reason for hesitating to associate it with prescriptive systems. In particular, if male ego's father had married his FBD, in accord with the preference, ego's FFBS would be his MB (in such a case, genealogical FFBD = genealogical MB), and therefore ego's FFBSD would also be his MBD [*see* Fig. 9.3(b)]. Because she counts as a patrilateral parallel cousin (a classificatory FBD) as well as a matrilateral cross cousin, a male ego can argue that he would be following the preference in marrying her. Similarly, if the marriages in the +1 generation had been reciprocal, that is, if two male patrilateral parallel cousins had exchanged sisters, then ego's FZ would have married ego's MB, their children being ego's cross cousins [*see* Fig. 9.3(c)]. However, because FZ would then also be MFBD, and MB also FFBS (both of whom are parallel kin types), their children can be seen as MFBDC and FFBSD – that is, as ego's second parallel cousins. In addition, if ego's FB had also married his FBD, this woman might well be a sister of ego's mother, which would make his own FBD also MZD. Even in these cases, however, it is likely that the ties through ego's FB are the ideologically stressed ones in the society concerned.

Such peculiarities do not mean that FBD marriage can be reduced to cross-cousin marriage or in any way be seen as a variant of it, because all systems of the latter entail quite different terminological and systematic consequences, as well as presuppositions, one of which is a prohibition on marrying any parallel cousin (*see* chapters 6–8). Nonetheless, this mixing of cross and parallel kin types makes the definition of such systems in specific genealogical terms even more arbitrary or (which amounts to the same thing) ideological, because relationships with a supposed parallel cousin can often be traced through a number of different genealogical paths (this problem is compounded if the preference or practice concerns second or third, and so on, rather than first parallel cousins).

FBD marriage also differs from prescriptive systems at the model level. Diagrams of the latter always express the intermarriage of opposite-sex sibling pairs in different descent lines in some variation or other, and they need not show same-sex collateral equivalents at all, nor multiple symbols for any kin type. Such diagrams also express the exogamy of the descent lines, something which will normally be reflected in the exogamy of spouse-exchange groups as regards the real system. Diagrams of such models can be extended indefinitely through any number of generations and still retain their shape, because the number of male and female symbols needed to show each marriage remains the same, each symbol representing one kin type, someone who is at once spouse to one ego and sibling to another. Such diagrams are purely representative, and despite their frequent use of genealogical symbols, they do not show a true genealogy.

A diagram consisting of *same-sex* sibling pairs who, of course, do not intermarry, although their children do (as with FBD marriage), differs in all these respects. Even in its purest form, it consists not of a series of separate descent lines, but of one hypothetical descent *group* which by definition must always include some same-sex collaterals and which assumes ever-greater collateral extent the further back or forward in time one goes [*see* Fig. 9.3(c)]. It therefore cannot be constructed in exactly the same way in every generation, and it would assume a different shape altogether if extended into the following generations. This is because symbols for certain kin types would very soon have to be duplicated in a way that is never necessary with diagrams of prescriptive systems. Moreover, it is not possible to take advantage of an equivalence between lineal and parallel kin (for example, F = FB), as is the case with any prescriptive model, because the model of FBC marriage depends crucially on their distinction (F ≠ FB). Descent-line endogamy is assumed (again reflecting reality) so that, unlike

Crow-Omaha models, the system is bounded, with alternative genealogical paths between all referents. The female symbols, however, though necessary to show each marriage, are redundant to the purpose of extending the diagram into further generations. There is thus an imbalance between male and female symbols compared with a prescriptive system. In the latter, two male and two female symbols are needed to show each marriage whereas, with FBC marriage, three males and one female are needed (male and female egos + F + FB): thus symbols do not invariably appear as spouse and sibling to different referents simultaneously. Indeed, attempts to make them do so merely render the diagram even more unwieldly than it will be already if several generations are shown. Consequently, even at the model level, the diagram comes to resemble less an abstract system of classification than an actual genealogy.

Thus as with Crow-Omaha systems, FBC marriage really lies near the limit of what is analytically definable. At the model level, both sorts of system – or really pseudo-system – suffer by comparison with the greater formal neatness of prescriptive systems, though for different reasons: Crow-Omaha models are unbounded, those of FBC marriage irregular. This does not render the elements from which they have been composed ethnographically invalid, but it does suggest that in neither case is social practice reifiable as a social system, whether indigenously or analytically.

1 0

The Meaning of Kinship

We have seen that many, though by no means all, non-Western societies conceive of themselves as being wholly composed of kin – at least, everyone in the society is referred to and addressed by kin term, even though their exact relationship, even in the society's own terms, may be unknown or uncertain. The West, however, has progressively diluted the circle of kin, recognizing most of society as both non-kin and non-affines. Although it is possible to identify extended families and kindreds in some parts of Europe, fully developed descent systems are rare; positive marriage rules have no place; only the remoter cousins among kin may be marriageable; and imperatives other than category (wealth, power, romantic love, simple companionship, mere opportunity) direct choice of spouse (of course, these may be influential in any society, including those with positive marriage rules). The family has progressively decreased in size in modern times, partly because fewer children are being born, and partly because of the increasing number of one-parent families. This is due in its turn to increased rates of divorce and illegitimacy, but for women in some Western circles it has become acceptable, even a goal in itself, to raise children without a resident male (also a feminine goal in some African societies). This is one aspect of another modern tendency, namely the questioning of marriage as an institution as such, which has also led to many couples living together and raising children without entering into any legal commitment with one another (the state may nonetheless enforce such commitments subsequently, for example, by allowing partners rights in each other's property upon their separation). In general, therefore, an increasing number of kin have been defined out of kinship altogether and placed in different categories of relationship that do not refer to kinship at all.

Pseudo-kinship

In some circumstances, conversely, people may be defined *into* kinship, as in institutions such as godparenthood or blood-brotherhood or more generally **ritual kinship** (sometimes **spiritual kinship** in respect of Christian societies). These use an idiom of kinship to create or symbolize relationships between particular individuals or groups within the society who are not related by what the society normally regards as kinship. They may come into existence between partners of either equal (for example, friend-friend) or unequal (such as patron-client) status, and sometimes take place between different descent groups or different ethnic or religious groups. They usually entail marriage prohibitions between the partners themselves, and often between members of their respective families and/or wider kin groups; and claims to inheritance may also be excluded. They tend to exist only where kinship in the more usual sense continues to be important, and to disappear where the significance of such kinship diminishes, as in parts of the West discussed above. In other words, they do not replace kinship but supplement it. They may be considered in part a further aspect of the phenomenon whereby certain societies seek to bring all their members into the universe of kin, though they are by no means absent from societies which have other modes of association too. The concept of ritual or ceremonial kinship therefore relates to the indigenous recognition that the kinship involved is different from that which the society recognizes as 'real' kinship and has to be created deliberately (through ritual, for example). This has nothing to do with the gap that almost inevitably exists between the indigenous view and the objective, scientific view of relatedness already discussed in chapter 1.

Ritual kinship is also to be distinguished from phenomena

such as adoption and fostering, where parental roles *vis-à-vis* one or more children are taken over either temporarily or permanently by different individuals or families from the children's natal families (*see* chapter 3). Such cases are sometimes called **fictive kinship**, though, like **pseudo-kinship**, this is often used simply as a synonym of 'ritual kinship'. 'Pseudo-kinship' is also found as a global term for all these phenomena, in which sense it is adopted here.

New Reproductive Technologies

Another, essentially modern aspect of the manipulation of kinship is the development of new reproductive technologies, which are designed to circumvent problems of infertility and detrimental genetic inheritance, but which also have the effect of fragmenting the accepted roles of fatherhood and/or motherhood between distinct persons. As we have seen, this fragmentation is not in itself either new or rare: anthropology has long had to make a basic distinction between pater and genitor, that is, between biological and social fatherhood, and there is a similar, if less commonly made, distinction between mater and genetrix (*see* chapter 2). It is also relatively familiar through step-relationships and adoption. The situation introduced by the development of new reproductive technologies however, is rather more complicated. There are three basic methods, all with significant variations. The first is artificial insemination of the prospective mother by either the husband (for example, if a physical disability prevents intercourse) or by a donor (for example, in cases of infertility). The second is *in vitro* fertilization (literally 'in-glass fertilization', as opposed to *in vivo* fertilization, or fertilization through sexual intercourse), or the production of so-called 'test-tube babies'. Again, this may use the semen of either the father or a donor, but the eggs may be donated also (or instead) if the mother is incapable of producing any. Lastly, there is surrogate motherhood, in which a female third party is commissioned by the husband and wife to carry an embryo to term on the latter's behalf. Again, there are numerous variants, depending on the source of semen and eggs, either or both of which may come from the respective parents or be donated. Technology may be circumvented altogether by the simple expedient of having the father impregnate the surrogate mother directly, in which case the former's wife can only ever be the mater of the child.

While the intention of all three basic methods is to produce children in circumstances where this is difficult or impossible by normal means, the effect is to cause parenthood to be shared with individuals outside the marriage or other stable partnership. Artificial insemination by donor produces a clear distinction between the genetic father and the social father. Depending on the exact circumstances, *in vitro* fertilization might produce a situation in which neither social parent is the genetic parent (if both sperm and eggs are donated) or only one of them is (if there is only one donation).

Surrogate motherhood can lead to an even more complicated situation, in which the social mother (that is, the commissioning mother) is one individual, the provider of the egg another, and the carrying mother a third. In addition, of course, the semen may be donated rather than coming from the social or commissioning father, involving five persons altogether. No doubt this is an extreme situation: in practice, some of these roles are likely to be conflated. The conflation of provider of the egg and bearer of the embryo, leaving only the separation of social and genetic motherhood, is not restricted to this technology (for example, stepmotherhood). It is the situation in which the provider of the egg is different from the bearer of the child that seems truly novel though, in fact, there are embryologies in the non-Western world which separate the source of the child from its bearer: for example, the child may be thought to enter the mother as or through a spirit, or the father may be defined as the sole source of new lives.

At present, therefore, the new reproductive technologies are a 'problem' for the essentially Western societies that have developed them rather than for other societies in the world, though this situation may change. They have led to questions being raised in Western societies of who the real parent is, the provider of the genetic material or the carer of the child after it is born, and also whether the child will develop complexes over its identity later in life. This is true whatever the method chosen, but the dilemma is perhaps most acutely felt with surrogate motherhood. Related to the question of parenthood is another question concerning the legitimacy of the children if the definition of who their parents are disregards the marriage of two of the candidates – if, for example, the surrogate mother, not the commissioning mother, is recognized in law or by society as the true mother.

Anthropology cannot take a moral position on these issues, but it can point out that there seem to be no problems of this sort inherent in more conventional cases of the fragmentation of parental roles, for example, step-parenthood or adoption. Although such practices are subject to cultural stereotypes, such stereotypes do not invariably apply in reality. Different dilemmas have been identified concerning succession and inheritance in cases where widows are fertilized by their dead husband's frozen sperm, another modern technical possibility. Should succession order be birth order, or the order in which sperm was produced by the husband, given that this technique conceptually separates the two? Again, the anthropologist can point out that variation in rules of succession and inheritance in the world generally show that a culturally imposed solution is perfectly possible. And this is indeed the anthropologist's basic message in all these cases: whatever science says or does, it will be society, acting through the law or public opinion, that will decide which definitions of kinship are acceptable. Indeed, in muddying conventional definitions of parental roles, science has virtually assured itself of social intervention, which it seems to welcome anyway.

Although at present confined to the West – where they are anyway restricted to a small percentage of the population – it is also interesting to contemplate the spread of such techniques to other parts of the world which have different conventional ideas about the kinship than the West. For example, a society which denied the mother any essential role in the creation of a new life might well find surrogate motherhood less problematic than one which saw her as wholly responsible for it. This is another argument for the view that responses to what appear to be culturally neutral scientific techniques are inevitably culturally specific, produced by and for the societies in which these techniques are being carried out.

'Sex-change operations', in which gender is changed through an operation, may also lead to a change and fragmentation of roles, if, for example, those undergoing such changes have been married and have children in their care. Also challenging for conventional ideas of kinship is the increasing acceptability of gay marriages in some countries, and of the possibility that same-sex couples may acquire children through adoption (they may anyway have children in some cases by virtue of a previous heterosexual marriage or relationship). Like the new reproductive technologies, if for different reasons, such arrangements call conventional notions of parenthood into question, though inheritance and succession for the children are perhaps more easily subsumable under concepts similar to step-parenthood and adoption in the society concerned.

From Kinship to Contract

The development of phenomena such as the fragmentation of parental roles through new reproductive technologies and same-sex succession through adoption raises the possibility of a society in which relationships need no longer be defined at all in ways that make explicit reference to kinship, of a society which therefore does not need to rely on conventional procreative methods for its continuity. Although a society formed exclusively in this way would be an innovation, however, human society has a long history of relationships formed in other ways than kinship, namely through informal associations or networks and formal contractual obligations. These, of course, are alternatives to kinship, and, while they may push back its boundaries, they have not so far been able to eradicate it entirely. They may receive conscious metaphorical expression in terms of kinship (for example, a priest as 'father'; the image of a king as 'father of the nation'), but their basis essentially lies outside it. The range of possibilities is considerable, but it includes friendship, relations between patron and client, lord and vassal, government and citizen, employer and worker, teacher and student, officer and soldier – and also relations between fellow citizens, soldiers, students, work-mates, and so on – age-grades or age-sets, religious associations or communities, and so on. To dwell on this further, however, would mean leaving the world of kinship behind us completely.

Cultural Approaches to Kinship

The emphasis in this book has been on formal and definitional aspects of kinship, which have dominated the subject traditionally in both analysis and description; they are also the ones that seem to give the student the most problems. Somewhat opposed to these, however, are so-called 'cultural' approaches, which concentrate less on social morphology than on the meanings given to kinship through metaphor, symbols, and so on. The roles expected of particular relatives, perceptions of their closeness or distance to ego, how one addresses them, the content of one's relationship with them, how this content varies between, say, affinity and consanguinity, are some of the topics cultural approaches address. Further, some of these approaches see culture as a system of meanings amenable to analysis every bit as rigorous as that of the more formal approaches, and the method has been used with reference to Western kinship, precisely the location of a supposedly scientific view of kinship that is culturally neutral. Using such methods, it has been possible to show that popular notions of kinship in the West frequently deviate from this scientific norm (*see* chapter 1).

This position is concerned above all to argue that kinship is a social or cultural matter, not a biological one, and that even the genealogical methods used by other anthropologists rarely correspond to indigenous values, even in the West, where they are supposed to be dominant. Some anthropologists have developed this into a denial that there is any separable domain of kinship, and even a denial that kinship exists at all. For some, kinship is merely an idiom, pure form to which only factors such as economics, politics or ritual can give any content. For others, the very cultural variation in what is conventionally defined as kinship is enough to deny that there is any such thing. In this view, the term itself has use as a rough means of indicating what one is going to be discussing but, as an analytically rigorous category, it is meaningless. None of this has discouraged other anthropologists from using it or studying what it represents.

Other cultural approaches concentrate on the cultural construction of the person, for example, the idea that bone comes from patrikin, flesh or blood from matrikin, or that a woman changes her own substance for that of her husband's on marriage, or that any individual may contain both male and female aspects, differentially combined. This has led in turn to enquiries into the anthropology of the body, which may not be seen as a bounded whole in all societies, nor as permanently marked by gender. Male and female substances may be seen as transformations of one another (for example, breast milk and semen). Notions of affinity and consanguinity may also be fused or refocused through, for example, a greater concentration on the nearness or remoteness of relationships instead.

Gender

There has also been an increasing tendency to recognize that the ways in which women view kinship may differ markedly from those of men, whose models anthropologists have traditionally found more accessible and have therefore mostly reproduced. Although the role differences most societies give to men and women have always been glaringly evident, and female-focused phenomena, such as matrilineal descent and brideprice, exhaustively studied, the assumption that women necessarily have the same view of these aspects as men has had to be abandoned. Thus gender as a separable topic has clear implications for the study of kinship, as much as for questions of symbolism, knowledge and power. The view of women as objects, subject to the control of men, has also had to be revised, more attention than formerly being given to their capabilities as subjects, creating their own meanings, and having influence in matters of kinship (such as over marriage choices for themselves or their children). Although women are still objects of affinal exchange in many societies, they are not as powerless as many male models suggest. Finally, there is a recognition that women have their own sociality, which interacts with the sociality of men without necessarily being dominated by it. The previous tendency to see all women as identifiable either with nature (as opposed to the 'maleness' of culture) or with the domestic sphere (as opposed to the public and collective sphere of men) has also had to be heavily qualified.

Ethnicity, Identity and Kinship

Finally, it has become increasingly appreciated that kinship can enter into the formation of a range of other identities. First, ethnic groups frequently define themselves through an idiom of shared descent reaching back into the past, perhaps to the origins of time, something which may be as important as a shared language, territory and culture. Secondly, types of family or other kinship grouping, marriage patterns, affinal alliance system and so on may not only have relevance for the generation of an interior world view and morality but also function to distinguish one ethnic group from another (for example, the presence or absence of cross-cousin marriage). Thirdly, ties of kinship may define individuals in different ways, depending on the nature of the tie, and they may also be opposed, or at least balanced, by other ties of a non-kinship kind. This appreciation is ultimately derived from cultural approaches, though they have increasingly had to recognize the fluidity with which different and competing modes of identity are pursued.

The Continuing Significance of Kinship

Kinship therefore remains relevant in all societies with regard to their morphology and continuity, and the meanings they create for themselves. There is nonetheless considerable variation in the ways in which different societies define and operationalize kinship so that, at the greatest level of detail, each society is likely to seem unique. To a set of frequently occurring concepts, none of which is essential, one must therefore add many cultural representations to arrive at each society's view of its own kinship system, on which its own identity may in turn depend. It is this that justifies cultural approaches, whether analytical or descriptive, as well as formal analysis and comparison. And it is the continuing relevance of kinship, finally, that will ensure that anthropologists will continue to have to give it attention, no matter what their individual theoretical orientations may be.

Part II
Theories of Kinship

11

The Significance of Kinship in Anthropology

Kinship has been of interest to anthropology throughout the history of the subject. Although the French explorer J. Lafitau included kinship in his description of the customs of native peoples in the Americas in the early eighteenth century, it was really the American lawyer, Lewis Henry Morgan, who established it as an intrinsic part of the discipline towards the end of the last century. Since then, many of the leading figures in anthropology have made their names at least partly through their writings on kinship – for example, Bronislaw Malinowski, W. R. R. Rivers, Raymond Firth, Arthur Radcliffe-Brown, Meyer Fortes, E. E. Evans-Pritchard, Jack Goody, Edmond Leach, Claude Lévi-Strauss, Louis Dumont, Rodney Needham and Marilyn Strathern – while in America Alfred Kroeber, Robert Lowie, George Murdock, Ward Goodenough, Harold Scheffler and David Schneider have all followed, in various ways, in Morgan's footsteps. Why is this? The basic reason is that kinship forms a main, if not the most important, organizing feature in the sorts of society the anthropologist has traditionally been most interested in. These are typically small-scale societies which lack a class system or other hierarchical structure, which live principally by subsistence farming, pastoralism or hunting and gathering, which are technologically simple, and whose world views are more usually characterized by beliefs in spirits and powers than by world religions.

It is not that anthropology has ignored kinship in larger-scale, more stratified societies, but its study is often something added on as an afterthought, if it is there at all. Even in anthropology, there is a lot one can say about modern societies without broaching the subject of kinship at all. Generally, this is much less possible with smaller-scale societies, simply because kinship enters into all sorts of things that a larger-scale society would handle differently.

Sir Henry Maine's distinction (1861) between status and contract as the bases on which societies are organized has therefore not lost its relevance. For Maine, a contemporary of Morgan, status here meant primarily kinship status, that is, a status one was born into. Societies organized mostly or entirely on the basis of kinship, in which one's role depends on the kinship categories into which one falls, were distinguished from societies where this gives way, at least in part, to links made between individuals on other grounds, such as fealty, agreement to act in a certain capacity, and so on. For example, the relationship might be that of ruler and subject, lord and serf, employer and worker, trader and customer and so on. This is not a completely neat division: for example, the notion of subject or citizen, which Maine placed under contract, is often dependent on one's birth. The two types are, therefore, ideal types, and most societies are likely to have a mixture of status and contract, not least because all societies have some sort of kinship. But the distinction has remained basically sound and sometimes appears in other forms; for example, Mauss's distinction (1938) between the role one plays in a kinship system and the modern concept of the person as one who is basically autonomous and therefore free to enter into contracts with others.

For Durkheim (1893), this was broadly the difference between segmentary societies, such as those with clan systems, which had 'mechanical solidarity', and societies in which the division of labour was operative, that is, they had 'organic solidarity'. With mechanical solidarity, the parts were all of the same kind (for example, clans or clan segments) and they simply duplicated one another: because they all had the same functions, it did not matter how many or how few there were (down to the number two, because of exogamy). In practice, this meant that the societies were based on kinship. With organic solidarity, on the other hand, the parts were of different kinds (such as different trades, different political and jural institutions), and they complemented each other: society could not function unless all were present.

Another question is the distinction between biological and social approaches to kinship. The biologist sees kinship primarily as a network of genetic connections and relationships, in so far as these can be determined. Cultural and social factors tend to be left out of consideration except in the most general way: for example, marriage as an institution is of less importance than mating as a means of procreation. For the social anthropologist, on the other hand, it is precisely the cultural and social factors that take priority, especially where these are specific to the society being studied. This is not to deny that kinship also has a biological dimension, and some anthropologists, such as Ernest Gellner (for example, 1957, 1960), have certainly sought to give this factor equal weight, arguing that what most anthropologists study in practice is the way these two dimensions, the social and the biological, are linked.

But as Dumont puts it [1971: 30, my translation]:

> The decisive answer to this trend has long been that the biological aspect is universal and cannot be the basis of observed differences, which are, let us remember, considerable, according to the type of society or culture – differences which appear immediately as conventional, 'arbitrary', in a word social, relevant to culture, not to nature, as Lévi-Strauss would say. [And further] ... all societies ground kinship to some extent on a biological given, but what makes them societies is the way in which they move away from this given, interpreting it and modifying it, and not the biological residue which remains in all their constructions.

Moreover, even the supposedly biological view has been argued to consist in academic or at least intellectual recensions of what originated as European folk models, such as the representation of descent through the image of a tree (Bouquet 1996), the notion that cognatic kinship is more 'natural' than unilineal descent (Needham 1969: 165; Strathern 1992: 68 ff.), and the definition of incest as illicit relations with close kin only.

For example, in most modern European societies, it is normally thought that men and women play an equivalent if different role in the creation of new life through their children, and indeed that children need a mother and a father when growing up. The former view clearly has roots in scientific reality, and, although it may be expressed differently in ordinary Western discourse, it also conforms to a widespread folk model. Elsewhere, however, one parent may be seen as relatively or absolutely more responsible for procreation than the other. In some societies, the father may simply 'open the way' for the child to be born, as among the Trobriand Islanders studied by Malinowski, who have matrilineal descent, though there has been much controversy over how far they are ignorant of paternity as such. On the other hand, the mother may be regarded as merely the vessel in which the father plants his seed, he alone being responsible for the new life that is born. This view is often encountered in strongly patriarchal societies, such as China. These sorts of view are not necessarily obvious from other factors in the society, for example the mode of descent: among another matrilineally structured group, the Bemba of central Africa, children are said to be given to women by their husbands. Thus, the mode of recruitment to social groups does not necessarily tell us anything about theories of birth and conception. A further example is belief in someone's rebirth in his or her grandchild – for example in central India or peoples of the Amazon basin – beliefs that do not conflict with the idea of children being born from their *parents*.

All this shows that theories of birth and conception vary widely, and that each forms part of a distinct cultural tradition. They are, in short, culturally determined. The anthropologist's task is to understand these representations in their social context and to describe both accurately, not to reduce them to a common standard, because this may well be exclusively biological and will almost certainly be Western in orientation.

Another question is whether kinship should be defined substantively, that is, as a matter of separate, concrete entities, or relationally, that is, with regard to the respective positions of individuals within a whole system. Broadly speaking, the former trend is identified with parts of the British school from the 1930s to the 1960s, reaching its apogee in the work of Meyer Fortes and his pupil Jack Goody, both of whom worked mainly in West Africa. For example, clans and lineages were defined in themselves, in terms of who belonged to them and what functions – possession of property, ancestor cults and so on – they performed. This was the Africanist model par excellence. In France, however, it became more common to concentrate on the links between clans and lineages made by marriage. These often had a definite regularity, especially in many Asian societies, leading them to be seen as alliances, often long term and lasting into succeeding generations. This was demonstrated forcefully by Lévi-Strauss in his great work *The Elementary Structures of Kinship* (1969). Lévi-Strauss based himself on written sources and also made fruitful use of the idea of exchange, drawing for this purpose on Mauss's work on the gift (1966). He was closely followed by Louis Dumont, based on fieldwork in south India (1953, 1983). This essentially French model, variously described as structuralist and holistic, proved more suitable for parts of the world outside Africa, especially parts of Asia, Indonesia, Australia and, with modifications, South America. It was followed by certain British anthropologists, in particular Edmond Leach and Rodney Needham. There was a tendency, however, for both schools to try to invade each other's territory, in the sense of applying models developed in one part of the world to others. This gave rise to many long and sometimes bitter controversies between what became known respectively as descent theory and alliance theory (*see* further, chapter 12).

Another continuing question has been what kinship consists of. It is common here to make a basic distinction between three different sorts of relation: descent (that is, vertical links between different generations); siblingship (that is, links between brothers and sisters); and affinity (that is, links by and through marriage). The first two, being based on what we would call blood ties, are often called relations of consanguinity, a word roughly meaning 'of same blood'. In much earlier British anthropology, including that of the descent theorists, there was a tendency to exclude marriage ties from the definition of kinship and to see it as consisting of ties of consanguinity alone. This effectively limited it to ties within the family, kindred and descent groups. It was the approach favoured by Radcliffe-Brown, as well as by Fortes and Goody, and some American writers such as Harold Scheffler. It is opposed to most

French anthropological writing, which tends to see kinship, or *parenté*, as including marriage too, kinship in the narrower sense of descent and siblingship being *consanguinité*. More recently, this practice has influenced English usage, which has increasingly come to include all relations of marriage in with 'kinship'.

The earlier association in Britain of kinship with consanguinity alone did not mean that British anthropologists denied the social nature of kinship, or that they tried to reduce it to purely biological facts. It did, however, strengthen their tendency to see kinship as a matter of substance rather than as a set of relationships, or rather, perhaps, to stress ties within clans, lineages and families at the expense of those between them. This impoverished somewhat the idea of a kinship *system* in their work, because the idea of ties or links of any sort was less important to them than the view of a clan or family as an entity in itself. This tendency is especially strong with Fortes and Goody: Radcliffe-Brown and Evans-Pritchard recognized the interdependence of different parts of the system. For the latter, however, in his work among the Nuer of the Sudan (1940, 1951), this was still mainly a matter of the interdependence of different parts of the same clan itself, that is, between clan segments (*see* chapter. 12). Only Radcliffe-Brown among this school recognized the importance of marriage to some extent, though even he remained tied to a view of kinship primarily as consanguinity.

A final question is the relationship of the kinship system, however defined, to the social system in general. Most anthropologists would recognize religion, politics, economics and so on, as separate domains from kinship proper. The question here becomes, is the kinship system of the same order as these other domains? John Beattie, for example, an Africanist, maintained that kinship was merely an idiom through which these other domains operated (1964). Thus, for example, economics is a matter of such things as co-operation in working land and the transmission of property after death, which in traditional society involves relatives, in that brothers might own land and farm together, inheritance might go from father to son and so on. For Beattie, it was only through such activities that kinship became apparent at all. Few, however, have accepted this view, especially, perhaps, those who see kinship as a matter of classification (an explicit critique is Schneider 1964). In societies organized principally on the basis of kinship, relationships of kinship are bound to have these other dimensions, political, economic, even religious (the pursuance of ancestor cults, for example). This does not of itself mean that kinship cannot be identified as a system in its own right, though the level at which one does identify it might well be more abstract.

For the structuralist, the very separation of domains in this fashion is wrong. It is to juxtapose things side by side, an approach that logically goes together with a view of social life which stresses substance over relation. In this view, society is not a collection of bits and pieces, of traits such as a particular sort of clan, family, marriage system, religion, myth, and so on, but a functioning whole, the parts of which are strictly interdependent. In this sense, Radcliffe-Brown was a structuralist, well known for his analogy of society as an organism, in which all the parts worked together. Yet he was also a functionalist, like Fortes and Goody, who saw social harmony and equilibrium as the goals of social life. In producing this harmony, the functioning of this organic kinship system was all-important. Another who, to some extent, bridged the divide between the two tendencies was Evans-Pritchard. As we have seen (*above*), although he certainly stressed the importance of viewing the kinship system as a whole and of taking note of the position of each element within it, his structuralism was largely a matter of balancing the different parts of the Nuer lineage or clan system against one another. He also virtually ignored the kinship terminology, that is, the classification of kin within the system. The structuralism of these two figures was therefore compromised to some extent by the importance they placed on descent and the family over marriage ties and classification, leading them to neglect vital aspects of the kinship system taken as a whole.

We see here the strong influence of Durkheim on Radcliffe-Brown, who did most to introduce Durkheim's work to English-speaking anthropology, as well as on Evans-Pritchard, and through him Fortes. In France, however, Durkheim's successors had moved on, starting with his nephew Marcel Mauss, who increasingly stressed the importance of studying societies as wholes, developed an important theory of exchange and recognized the importance of classification. All these aspects were to be influential with Lévi-Strauss and Dumont, and with the former's British followers such as Leach and Needham. For all of them, kinship systems were systems of classification and therefore of meaning, not machines or functioning organisms. This meant giving equal prominence to alliance through marriage as to descent. In the case of Lévi-Strauss, indeed, the idea of an underlying system of thought, of which these were all merely surface phenomena, was fundamental.

1 2

Theories of Descent

Theories of descent have played a vital part in the history of anthropological theory, though for the most part, they have concentrated on unilineal descent. Cognatic descent, largely disregarded in earlier anthropology, had to wait a century before receiving much in the way of theoretical attention (q.v. chapter 2, above).

Many early anthropologists writing in the 1850s, 1860s and 1870s, such as Morgan, McLennan and Bachofen, recognized both forms of unilineal descent, matrilineal and patrilineal. However, they saw them as characterizing whole societies, which they then placed in an evolutionary sequence, matrilineal coming before patrilineal. For all these figures, the earliest stage of society actually entailed 'primitive promiscuity', in which there were no rules of marriage or descent at all. This situation led to emphasis being placed on links between mother and child because, whereas the identity of the father could never be known for certain, that of the mother always was. Hence, the earliest stage of organized human society proper was matrilineal or, in the jargon of the time, matriarchal. Only later did it become patrilineal or patriarchal, a change linked in some authors to the invention of the institution of marriage. Morgan was influenced in this view of primitive promiscuity leading to matriarchy by his experience of the Seneca Iroquois, who were organized into matrilineages (1877). Bachofen (1861) was struck by reports of existing matrilineally organized societies in contemporary travel literature. McLennan (1865) was influenced by extensive reports of simulated bride-capture at weddings, which he interpreted as a survival of the actual capture of females under primitive promiscuity. For McLennan, primitive promiscuity and matriarchy were especially found in nomadic hunting and gathering societies. It was agriculture and settlement that led the change to patriarchy, because men typically undertook the farming. As a result, property also became important, and with it inheritance. These ideas were adopted by Morgan, from whom they were taken up by Marx and Engels, who made them the basis of their historical account of the rise of property and, later, of capitalism.

McLennan also introduced the concept of exogamy, that is, the requirement to marry out of the group. This has remained important in anthropology in respect of how different descent groups are distinguished from one another and also how they are interrelated in the same society. Descent groups are defined for many anthropologists by their exogamy. For Lévi-Strauss (1969) and his followers, this also forms the basis of their relationships with one another. In this view, descent groups are deficient only in that they have to obtain their spouses from elsewhere, a direct result of their rules of exogamy. Breaking these rules is often seen as incest, even where distant relations are concerned.

Incest and exogamy apart, anthropologists today generally accept no part of these early theories. In particular, it is most unlikely that human society evolved without some order relating to marriage and descent already in existence. Even our closest primate relatives live in social groups which can often be reduced to some form of at least statistical order. In effect, such theories are the early anthropological equivalent of the initial state of nature proposed by philosophers such as Hobbes and Rousseau, from which human society came about through contract. This is not an approach that has practical use for anthropologists today, though it remains of interest to the history of the subject.

The idea of a general transition from matriarchy to patriarchy has also been discredited, though there are historical exceptions (for example, the Nayar of south India; Fuller 1976). Indeed, there is no agreed reason for the distinction, whether historically or theoretically, and it is no longer an anthropological preoccupation to find one. Though in a minority compared with their patrilineal or cognatic equivalents, many societies with matrilineal descent occur, often in pockets (for example, lacustrine central Africa, parts of north-east and south India, and south-central Vietnam).

There is also an objection to interpreting human history as a series of changes, each affecting the whole world at the same time apart from a few isolated 'survivals' from which that history can be reconstructed. The idea of survivals is generally doubted, partly because it takes no account of the possibility that some social groups may follow a certain way of life out of preference or necessity, not inertia. Also, it is no longer accepted, as it used to be, that, for example, Australian aborigines are representative of early humanity: they are just as much a part of contemporary humanity as ourselves.

Sir Henry Maine, another nineteenth-century writer, developed an opposite theory to Bachofen's (their respective works appeared in the same year, 1861). In Maine's view, society had always been patrilineal and patriarchal. He based his view on early historical evidences, which always indicated patriarchy, never matriarchy. He also rejected the idea of primitive promiscuity, seeing marriage as the basis of the family and, therefore, of human society. The family was under the authority of the father, as in the Roman *patria potestas*. In this, he was supported by Fustel de Coulanges (1864), a French scholar who taught Durkheim, and Edward Westermarck, a Finnish scholar (1891). Westermarck in particular maintained, against Morgan, that incest prohibitions and the institution of the family had always existed and that there had been no early stage of primitive promiscuity. Malinowski also gave a priority to the nuclear family in his more synchronic approach (1913). For Fustel de Coulanges, the family had developed into the patrilineal clan through the introduction of the worship of ancestors, from whom the clan was supposedly descended. Ancestor worship certainly provides descent groups with identity in many societies. Others, especially Emile Durkheim (1915) and his followers but also Sir James Frazer (1910), saw totemism as the original ritual basis for the existence of clans (for Durkheim, totemism was also the earliest form of religion). Maine was also one of the first to realize that descent *per se* can be modified by other forms of recruitment –

adoption, co-option and so on – that, in time, might take over from descent completely. This is the origin of his distinction between status and contract (*see* chapter 11).

By early in the twentieth century the matriarchal theory had effectively been abandoned, and the family was generally accepted as the basis, historically as well as contemporaneously, of human society. At the same time, it began to be recognized that clans and other descent groups were frequently linked to a particular territory, however they were organized in other ways. Radcliffe-Brown, writing about Australian societies in the 1930s (1930–31), explicitly made the link between descent and territory, using the term 'horde' almost interchangeably with 'clan'. This led some American anthropologists to challenge the idea of descent itself as a primary constituent of social groups. Alfred Kroeber, for instance, stressed residence and common economic activities (farming and so on). Robert Lowie (1920) and George Murdock (1949) turned the whole theory of descent around by claiming common residence as the basic factor, which gave rise to descent – that is, people did not live together because they were related by descent but were related by descent because they lived together. Kroeber's idea that territoriality is the basis of what are normally called descent groups has been taken up much more recently by Adam Kuper (1982), in an article that comes close to dismissing the idea of descent altogether. This is an extreme view, though it is clear that the anthropologist's traditional model of descent has to be modified in certain respects, as we shall see later.

One important innovation of the 1920s was W. R. R. Rivers's definition (1924: 85–8) of descent as membership of groups only, which should be distinguished both from the inheritance of property and from succession to office. This was because these various phenomena were not always transmitted in the same way. As a result, it is rarely appropriate to characterize a whole society as patrilineal, matrilineal or bilateral, as is still sometimes done. To operate effectively, however, continued Rivers, descent groups had to have clearly defined boundaries and membership. This meant that only unilineal descent groups could be considered genuine descent groups, because only they limited membership to birth in one line and only they were strictly exogamous. Unlike with cognatic descent, where membership was to some extent optional, in the case of unilineal descent, men and women could only be members of one descent group. Moreover, each group, however self-sufficient in other ways, needed other groups to provide it with spouses, because of the rule of exogamy. As we have seen (chapter 2), these differences are not really reliable ways of distinguishing unilineal and cognatic descent, which really differ from one another only through mode of descent. Nonetheless, many anthropologists, including Radcliffe-Brown, Meyer Fortes, Edmond Leach and Louis Dumont, have followed Rivers in seeing only unilineal descent as true descent, though not Raymond Firth and others who have had to deal with cognatic descent, nor Jack Goody in his work on West Africa.

For Radcliffe-Brown (1950; 1952: chapter 2), unilineal descent groups were the corporations on which social continuity depended in many societies, because they survived the individuals of which they were composed. As 'corporate groups', they were usually characterized by the possession of common property, common allegience to authority (chief or council) and common rituals. Radcliffe-Brown also saw descent groups as having functions, the chief of which was that they distributed rights and duties of all kinds to and among their members. This meant that they had to be readily identifiable from one another, as only unilineal descent groups were then thought to be. It also meant that descent gradually came to be combined with inheritance and succession, in opposition to Rivers's plea to keep these separate.

This trend reached its height in the work of Fortes and Goody. For Fortes (1945, 1953, 1959), who worked among the Tallensi of West Africa, descent groups formed the primary divisions in those societies that had them. Like Radcliffe-Brown, he considered descent groups to be corporate groups, surviving the lives of their members and often being concerned with common property at some level, whether this was tangible or something more like a cult. They were also conceived by Fortes as 'moral persons', in the sense that their unity gave them individuality in relation to one another, that is, they were collective individuals.

This sense of togetherness was supported by ritual and institutions, and its ultimate purpose was the maintenance and continuity of the social system as a whole. Furthermore, descent was significant in providing the link between the two different domains of social organization that Fortes defined (1945, 1949). While the family and kinship were matters of mainly private, day-to-day concern, descent concerned the clan and lineage system on a more occasional, but public basis. This was the distinction between the 'domestic' domain, which provided such things as food and shelter on a daily basis, and the 'politico-jural' domain, which was more concerned with inheritance, residence rules and exogamy. This distinction between the family and the clan also led to a distinction between filiation (ties between parents and children, which were necessarily bilateral, as well as between siblings) and descent (ties stretching back over generations, which in Tallensi society were unilineal). Finally, it meant that kinship was ultimately subsumed by descent, in that it was descent that united the domestic and jural domains, whereas kinship was confined to the domestic domain, that of the family, alone.

With Goody (1961; cf. Leach 1962), the tendency to link descent with inheritance becomes absolute: indeed, for him, descent exists only where property is inherited by succeeding generations down the line or lines of descent. Moreover, this does not necessarily mean property common to the clan, as for Fortes, but the property of individuals and/or families. The distinction between moral person and corporate group was not maintained by Goody, who recognized only the latter. In this way, Goody was able to advance a theory of double unilineal descent for some societies, that is, those that have different sorts of property being inherited. patrilineally and matrilineally. The problems with this can be seen in north India where, although most property – especially land and houses – goes from father to son, some property, in the form of clothes and jewellery, goes from mother to daughter. Descent as such, however, that is, the recognition of vertical ties, is patrilineal. This means that both sons and daughters are patrilineally linked to ancestors, whereas patrilineally transmitted property goes to sons only.

One controversy here has concerned the notion of complementary filiation, proposed by Fortes in particular (1953, 1959) and discussed critically by Leach (1957, 1960), who had worked in the very different society of the Kachin in Upper Burma (1951). This related not to the internal structure of descent groups or to how their segments were related, but to the relationships *between* them. For Leach, following Lévi-Strauss [1969 (1949)], this was a matter of ties created by marriage, a consequence of the rule of exogamy, which was seen as a defining quality of unilineal descent groups, at least at some level of segmentation. Moreover, the sorts of society that Leach and others were mainly interested in usually treated marriage as a means of creating enduring alliances between descent groups, sometimes running for generations. As a result, this theory came to be known as 'alliance theory' because it emphasized the ties of marriage alliance between descent groups rather than the latter's internal structure.

This theory opposed, and was opposed by, what came to be known as 'descent theory', that is, the work of Fortes, Evans-Pritchard and Goody in particular. Although they acknowledged that descent groups intermarried, the notion of exogamy, even as drawing a boundary round the descent group, was under-emphasized. What Fortes and Goody in particular preferred to stress in this context were the ties of complementary filiation that linked ego and his or her parent of the gender that does not carry the descent line. Thus in a society with patrilineal descent, ego has ties of descent with and through his father, but also ties of complementary filiation with, and implicitly through, his mother. The key to understanding this as an alternative to the theory of marriage alliance is that although ego's mother is the wife of ego's father and therefore must have come originally from a different descent group, by the rule of exogamy she is related to ego as a consanguine. Thus the spouse of the present generation becomes a parent for the next one. Ego's ties with his mother's patrilineal descent group in our hypothetical society therefore run through his mother, and have nothing to do with the marriage of ego's parents (except in so far as this legitimates the relation of filiation). In other words, where alliance theorists stressed marriage ties, descent theorists explained them by using descent and filiation. Alliance theorists saw society as a matter of relations, through marriage especially, between groups, whereas for descent theorists society was characterized by groups alone, which entailed notions of substance, including rights and duties, being transmitted via descent groups down the generations.

Another difference between descent theory and alliance theory relates to the sorts of data they examined. A distinction is often made between three different levels of data in respect of kinship: rules, which lay down how the individual in society should act; behaviour, or how he does actually act, especially whether in accordance with the rules or not; and kinship terminology, or in other words the ways in which kin are classified, that is, the terms one uses for different categories of kin, like father, son, uncle, and so on (for example Needham 1973). We shall go into more detail concerning the relation between these three levels of data in chapter 13. For the moment, we should simply register a few key trends. British descent theory tended to focus on the levels of rules and behaviour in explaining kinship systems. An account of a kinship system was seen in part as a matter of describing the behaviour of individuals in face-to-face interaction, assessing from this the extent to which they obeyed the rules of their society. Again, this was followed especially by Radcliffe-Brown, and taken up by his followers, including Fortes and Goody.

But as Dumont has pointed out, 'there are other things in a kinship system than simply interpersonal relationships.' In fact, alliance theorists increasingly came to the conclusion that kinship is ultimately a matter of classification, an assumption that led them to place the priority on the level of the terminology. This tendency reached its height with Rodney Needham, who has analysed more kinship terminologies than virtually anyone else. For him, kinship systems were to be classified principally through the categories in which they placed kin, though others, in particular Leach (1945, 1958) and Dumont (1953), also contributed here with key articles of their own. The significance of a kinship terminology is that it forms its own particular pattern, one which varies from society to society, though only within certain limits. More to the point here, it often has a particular significance in societies where alliances through marriage are more important than descent. For the descent theorists, in fact, terminology was a mere reflection of the levels of behaviour and rules. Even for Radcliffe-Brown, who recognized the importance of terminology, it was behaviour, or what he called attitudes, that were truly important, and these the terminology merely reflected. For alliance theorists, on the other hand, it was the key to the whole kinship system.

Another characteristic of lineage or descent theory was that it was no longer concerned with placing different sorts of descent group in an evolutionary sequence – indeed, it was not interested in history at all. What it was interested in was how the different elements that made up traditional societies were brought together and how they ensured stability and continuity. The time dimension was a matter, not of actual history or postulated trends in world history, but, if at all, of the process whereby societies solved changes of a domestic sort that they were repeatedly faced with, especially, perhaps, the births, deaths and marriages of their members. One aspect of this was the idea of the domestic cycle, that is, the process of development, decay and renewed development of the family, as its members grow old and die. Another development in the work of Radcliffe-Brown, Fortes, Evans-Pritchard and Goody was the theory of 'segmentary lineage systems'. This was applied to how descent systems behaved politically, especially in Africa, and was thought to have particular relevance to 'stateless' societies.

The distinction between state and stateless societies went back to Maine and Morgan. There were traditional, pre-colonial states in Africa, which were seen as having adminstrative bodies that were not based on descent. In stateless societies in Africa, on the other hand, politics was often a matter of the interrelationship of the segments of a descent system. The classic example was Evans-Pritchard's work among the Nuer of the Sudan (1940) where, although the segments of each descent group were potentially hostile to one another, order is nonetheless maintained. For example, while segments of lineages may have disputes among themselves, they combine when faced with the hostility of another lineage; similarly, different lineages will temporarily postpone their own conflicts when the clan of which they are all a part is threatened by another clan. The way a segment behaves therefore depends on the level of segmentation involved in any particular dispute. The model is dynamic, in the sense that it shows how the Nuer deal with internal conflicts, but it is not historical, because they always come back to the same point of equilibrium. As

Dumont points out (1973), whereas Fortes and Radcliffe-Brown had stressed the corporate descent group as a whole, Evans-Pritchard saw this as a contingent matter and stressed descent-group segments instead.

As we saw in chapter 11, Adam Kuper (1982) challenged the descent component in these models, arguing, largely on the basis of what Evans-Pritchard and Fortes themselves wrote, that the models existed only inside their own heads. This is a harsh view, though it is supported by ethnography from some parts of the world, such as New Guinea, where J. A. Barnes (1961) and others have shown that agnatic ties are typically supplemented by matrilateral and affinal ties and a degree of choice as to residence. This weakens the agnatic composition of the typical group. Yet it is undoubtedly true that many societies regard their links with the ancestors from whom they trace descent as important. Some anthropologists (for example, Harold Scheffler, 1966) have been led to regard descent as a matter of classification or categories rather than groups, an emphasis that also impinges on the question of kinship terminology, a main topic in the next two chapters.

1 3

Kinship Terminology and Affinal Alliance

Since Morgan, there have been many controversies in social anthropology concerning the nature and significance of kinship terminologies, most of which can be grouped under three basic themes: first, their relation to social structure (especially affinal alliance), secondly the extent to which they denote genealogical relationships rather than categories, and thirdly the nature of terminological change. The first two themes are treated in this chapter, the third in chapter 14.

Terminology and Social Structure

One of the things Morgan is most remembered for (1871, 1877) is his idea of the 'classificatory' terminology, merging some collateral kin with lineal kin on the basis of same-sex sibling equivalence rather than grouping all collateral kin together and separating them from lineal kin. He tried to account for this as the outcome of different types of mating, one of which was marriage in the modern sense, another 'primitive promiscuity'. But he also expressly saw kinship terminology as denoting blood relationships, an essentially Western, genealogical point of view – that is, different marriage patterns give rise to different genealogical links, and these to different terminological patterns. This was soon rejected by McLennan (1876) with reference to one of Morgan's main examples, the

classificatory Iroquois terminology. Although descent and inheritance implied genealogical reckoning on the matrilineal side, the
two sides of the terminology, patrilineal and matrilineal, had an
identical structure. Thus the Iroquois terminology did not reflect
their social structure, and, as a result, McLennan argued that kin
terms were simply 'salutations', a view that regards kin terms as
modes of address but ignores their use in reference.

Although McLennan opposed Morgan's view that kinship terminology was an outcome of the marriage system, he did not really
expand on his objections. The first to suggest a clear alternative was
Alfred Kroeber (1909), student of Franz Boas and, as such, both a
relativist and one whose idealist view of culture made much use of
the analogy of language. Kroeber's article was very short, but it
contained two points critical of Morgan. One was that there was no
absolute difference between that which Morgan had described as
'classificatory' and 'descriptive' terminologies: it all depended on
the cultural point of view of the observer. This led him to dismiss
the sort of typology that Morgan had advanced in favour of principles of relationship – age, sex, generation, and so on. This argument
of Kroeber's is actually based on a misreading of Morgan, to the
effect that classificatory differs from descriptive in that only the
latter is genealogical. In fact, to Morgan both sorts of system were
genealogical, the difference between them being in the actual pattern of genealogical links (cf. White 1958). This difference depended in its turn on the different sorts of marriage system that
were associated with each – that is, marriage created the genealogy
which the terminology expressed. In respect of the terminologies
themselves, then, the difference for Morgan was between those
that isolated lineal relatives from collateral ones and those that
merged them. Despite Kroeber, it has proved possible to erect
typologies for kinship terminologies, though in analysis it is often
necessary to apply them differentially within actual individual examples (for example, to different genealogical levels). Today, the
term 'classificatory' has come to be restricted to terminological
equations between lineal and collateral kin (F = FB; B = FBS, and
so on). Robert Lowie (1920) suggested replacing 'descriptive' with
'individualizing' as the opposite term.

Kroeber's second point was that kinship terminology is primarily an aspect of language, and that any connection it may have with social organization cannot be assumed but must be proved in each case. Unfortunately, here too, Kroeber made future trouble for himself by using the word 'psychology' in this connection, though he later made it clear (1952) that this word was ill chosen and that 'unconscious logic and conceptual patterning', as in the use of language, would have been preferable. The real implication of this second point, however, is that kinship terminologies form independent semantic systems that can be analysed as such, it being neither necessary nor possible to regard them as mere epiphenomena of the social structure.

The seeds of this position can be found in McLennan, but it is really Kroeber who must be credited with its explicit formulation. It is also found in later writers, most of whom are far more determinist in their general approach than Kroeber – there are similar aspects to Malinowski's work, for instance (1929), even though he was hardly a relativist like Kroeber. This was partly because, like Kroeber, he rejected the notion that kinship terminologies could be used to tell us about past institutions such as marriage systems (1930). In Britain and France, however this separation of kinship terminology and social structure was for a time resisted. Rivers (1914a, 1914b) was an early critic of Kroeber and a sympathizer of Morgan, especially of the latter's evolutionism, arguing in particular that where prescriptive terminologies were found without the marriage systems logically associated with them, the former should be considered survivals of a previous stage in which the latter existed too.

Radcliffe-Brown was also very critical of this 'conjectural history', but he supported Rivers and Morgan at least in seeing patterns of kinship terminology as reflecting social structure (1952: chapter 3). In his case, however, this meant not so much marriage as descent, that is, lineal unity and the 'unity of the sibling group', social attitudes and the attribution of status. For the American Murdock (1949), descent underlay kinship terminology even more explicitly.

But Kroeber's attitude also persisted in America. His anti-determinism is reflected in the relativism of Schneider, for instance (1962). Moreover, two groups who have taken up his view of kinship terminology as primarily linguistic are the componential analysts led by Ward Goodenough (1956) and the semantic analysts led by Harold Scheffler and Floyd Lounsbury (for example, Scheffler and Lounsbury 1971; Lounsbury 1956). They all launched their approaches in the same period as the Chomskyian revolution and other developments in linguistics, and there was a certain amount of cross-influence between the two disciplines at this time, though this did not prevent their different ultimate developments. But Goodenough was also influenced by Kroeber's position in another sense, in that he exploited the sorts of principles Kroeber had advocated in analysing kinship terminologies. Both these approaches treat kinship terminologies as systems of meaning in a very abstract sense and seek to reduce them to rigid logical principles. Most such work is ultimately of value in translating indigenous systems into analytical formulas rather than in understanding them in their own right (though their proponents would sharply disagree here). While Goodenough does give consideration to the informant's own meanings, this is not his ultimate aim, and in the hands of Lounsbury and Scheffler, the formal elegance of the model becomes progressively more important and the isolation of the data from any social or historical context more profound. In addition, Scheffler specifically excludes marriage systems as being of any significance in the formation of kinship terminologies, and he does not recognize prescriptive terminologies, that is, those with cognate-affine equations, as a separate class (for example, 1978).

In Europe, things took a rather different course in this period. In *The Elementary Structures of Kinship* (1969), Lévi-Strauss took the view that neither kinship terminology nor social structure determined the other, but that they were both aspects of the same underlying mode of thought. By this, he meant not the more or less tangible properties of Radcliffe-Brownian social structure – lineages, marriage classes, and so on – but the configurations of the collective consciousness, located ultimately in the human brain. More exactly, perhaps, kinship terminology and concomitant social structure were both cultural expressions of this consciousness. Moreover, for Lévi-Strauss it was marriage, or more precisely affinal alliance – namely the repetition of marriages over time – that was the significant element in social organization, not descent, as it had been for Radcliffe-Brown. Indeed, although recognizing the importance of terminologies in principle, Lévi-Strauss virtually ignored them in practice, mostly preferring to concentrate on the data of marriage rules in establishing the characteristics of particular kinship systems. In addition, he took from Mauss (1966) the notion of exchange and, in combination with exogamy, applied it to marriage to create a whole theory of affinal alliance. According to this theory, the incest taboo was the foundation of society because although its boundaries were culturally variable, it was essentially the negative counterpart to a principle of reciprocity: one's own group was required to forego its own women in marriage for the sake of giving them to another group and obtaining theirs in return. Just as Lévi-Strauss declined to give a priority to either terminology or alliance but regarded both as surface manifestations of a common underlying structure of thought, so too he declined to derive either incest from exogamy/exchange or vice versa in the generation of his theory.

The first position in particular led some to charge him with an evasion of the issues and an overall lack of clarity. This was especially so for Rodney Needham, who felt that Lévi-Strauss's distinction between prescription and preference, which was also that between model and reality for Lévi-Strauss, was inadequate, and frequently unclear (for example, Needham's Introduction to Lévi-Strauss 1969). Needham, however, was already encountering challenges in his own work on prescriptive systems, that is, the elementary structures with which Lévi-Strauss had been concerned. As with Lévi-Strauss, this has concerned the reworking of other people's data rather than the analysis of his own, and his problems concerned the definition of such systems.

Needham's early work was often taken as suggesting that a system was prescriptive if there was an explicit rule of cross-cousin marriage. If the terminology did not correspond to the alliance system, it was either because the former had changed to a greater degree than the latter in history, or else simply because the data were somewhere wrong. The latter device led to the charge, especially from Schneider (1962), that Needham was merely making the data fit a preconceived theory. As a consequence, the mismatches between kinship terminology and social structure still had to be adequately explained and, Schneider hinted, could not be. Schneider also protested at the view that prescription was essentially to do with marriageability – that it simply defined the marriageable category within the terminological system. To Schneider, this was a tautology: by definition, the only other categories in the system were non-marriageable, either because they fell in with bounds of incest rules, or else because they violated the prescription, so that to say that one must marry the prescribed category of kin is simply to say that one must marry a marriageable individual.

This eventually led Needham to clarify matters in his 1973 article 'Prescription', an article which is also partly a reply to Lévi-Strauss. In it, he distinguished three levels of analysis: terminology, rules and behaviour. Furthermore, he advocated applying the term 'prescription' to the former only and abandoning its use in respect of rules, that is, alliance, altogether. Thus increasingly, he saw terminology as a system of classification of linguistic character and as this alone, any connection with social structure being an open question necessitating independent proof in each case. In addition, Needham hints at the essentially unreflective way in which kinship terminology is actually used, owing to its linguistic character. Thus, here he approaches Kroeber's attitude to the significance of kinship terminology, though Needham is less completely dismissive of its social-structural implications. In fact, the only respects in which he parts company with Kroeber are in allowing the possibility of typologies, at any rate of the principles that organize terminologies, if not of whole terminologies themselves, and also in recognizing the possibility of historical changes in terminology.

Needham's article answered the points raised by Schneider, though he made no reference to the latter in doing so. In particular, prescription is implicitly recognized as necessarily a tautology at the level of rules, and it now becomes just a property of those terminologies that Lévi-Strauss termed elementary structures. Leach (1945) and Dumont (1953) foreshadowed Needham in seeing kinship terminology as a system in its own right (following Kroeber) in classic studies on the Kachin and Tamils respectively. However, they do not follow Kroeber and, implicitly, Needham in seeing kinship terminology as an aspect of language. Nonetheless, this approach obviates the search for sociological factors influencing change in kinship terminology, which tends to be invoked by those who see kinship terminology as an epiphenomenon of social structure (for example, Elman Service 1960). Needham's insistence on the separation of terminology and social structure is certainly pragmatic: given the frequent lack of fit in logical terms, it is appropriate to consider each separately before trying to move to a global view.

In this whole argument over the relationship between terminology and social structure, it is important to keep clear the distinction between prescription and non-prescription, or, in Lévi-Strauss's terms, elementary and complex structures, for in the former case it is possible to see a connection, at least logically and very often in reality, beween terminology and affinal alliance. Although many American schools of thought remain sceptical of this, for most European anthropologists the problem here is not so much the existence of a relationship but the exact form it takes. As we have seen, for Needham, the separation of the various levels of data is more an operational requirement than a matter of principle, as it is for, say, Scheffler or, in a different way, Schneider's cultural approach (1968). As for non-prescriptive or complex systems, the only connection between terminology and social structure seems to be the mere absence of prescription rather than any positive logical correspondence.

Genealogy versus Category

Although opposed to Morgan's evolutionism, Malinowski resembled him in taking an explicitly genealogical view of kin terms, though his view was that the closest genealogical specifications were the primary ones, all the other meanings of a term being metaphorical extensions (for example, 1929). This was not a matter of historical development but reflected the order in which the various meanings were learnt by the infant. This was partly the result of his belief in the primacy of the nuclear family, a belief that involves a degree of psychological reductionism: society is the outcome of basic human needs, psychological as well as physical, as expressed through the nuclear family. Malinowski's extensionist views were opposed first of all by Hocart (1937), who pointed out their inadequacy in arriving at the indigenous concept of what the terms mean, for the criteria on which this meaning was based were frequently different from the conventional European perspective. Much later, Leach, using Malinowski's own data from the Trobriands (1958), argued that it was the whole category, not a particular genealogical specification, that was the true meaning of the indigenous terms in that particular case. This view has been exploited especially by Needham and those who have followed him, and it is also implicit in Dumont's work.

Nonetheless, the extensionist viewpoint resurfaced in the 1950s in the American schools of componential analysis associated with Goodenough and semantic analysis associated with Lounsbury and Scheffler. As we have seen, these approaches are, strictly, distinct. The former is more concerned to describe the content of terms in respect of age, sex, generation, and so on, taking its cue from Kroeber. The latter focuses on 'equivalence', 'expansion' and 'reduction rules', which function as operators generating the specifications of a single term. Both, however, seek the most economical definitions, and this leads to a concentration on the minimal genealogical specifications, all others, as in Malinowski, being extensions. Indeed, we have also seen that for Scheffler, kinship is basically a matter of genealogy alone.

In reducing kinship to genealogy, Scheffler and Lounsbury also bear a resemblance to the work of Fortes, whose version of descent theory similarly relied on the nuclear family and minimal genealogical ties, although he was also keen to distinguish the familial, domestic domain from the politico-jural domain of descent groups (*see* chapter 11). Indeed, Scheffler has frequently supported Fortes in print against his detractors. From the point of view of the current debate, it can be argued that the most distant of the alliance theorists from the Schefflerian perspective is Dumont. In his work on Dravidian kinship in particular (1953, 1983), Dumont stressed the alliance aspect above all else, and he went on to reverse the main tendency of descent theory in that he saw certain consanguines – especially mother's brother – as primarily affinal relatives. His explicit statements here have not been followed even by all alliance theorists, many of whom prefer to see this and similar specifications as having a double aspect. Dumont's pronouncements are always linked very closely to specific sets of data, however, and in the present case he was careful to make it clear that he was talking of Dravidian kinship only. It is also important to note that, being very much under the influence of Lévi-Strauss early in his career (1953), he was concerned with the underlying pattern of the Tamil and allied terminologies, not with the analysis of a single terminology. Although his famous paper 'The Dravidian Kinship Terminology as an Expression of Marriage' (1953) is generally taken as being a discussion of a kinship terminology, it actually contains not a single indigenous kin term. Its point is rather that the terminological and affinal alliance patterns are linked. Lévi-Strauss himself, whose influence here Dumont was later to acknowledge, would almost certainly have made explicit the idea that both are really surface manifestations of a common underlying mental structure.

The main objection with a genealogical point of view is primarily that it is a Western one and not necessarily that which the people themselves employ. This has caused particular difficulties over what is meant by cross-cousin marriage. The ethnography sometimes seems to contradict itself in saying that there is a rule of MBD marriage but that statistically one's actual MBD is rarely in fact married. The solution will usually prove to be that the term for MBD covers a wider category than just this genealogical specification. That is to say, it is the whole category, not just the genealogical MBD, that is prescribed, and indeed such systems could scarcely work in any other fashion for the good demographic reason that not every male ego will have a real MBD (cf. Needham 1960a).

14
Typologies and Terminological Change

Some have felt that the contrast between prescriptive and non-prescriptive is not simply typological or related to the mechanical interaction between terminology and social structure – there may be a historical dimension too. This is a relatively modern phenomenon, despite the evolutionism of Morgan and Rivers, which was more concerned with using terminology to identify possible changes in other parts of the kinship system than with changes in terminology as such. Morgan's ideas in this respect were apparently developed hurriedly, almost as an afterthought, but Rivers in particular saw greater stability in kin terms when compared with marriage systems, and, as we have seen, he used this to trace historical changes in the latter. This was the 'conjectural history' that Radcliffe-Brown and Malinowski so much objected to, and so bitter were these attacks that anthropology and history in Britain largely parted company for a generation. From a more modern perspective, however, the main fault of Rivers and Morgan seems to reside in their tendency to see the terminologies themselves as necessarily stable.

In America, even though the dominant Boasian school of anthropology was also basically anti-evolutionist, historical approaches survived better than in Britain. A number of studies by Hallowell (1928), Eggan (1937) and Spoehr (1947) were largely concerned to link changes in kinship terminology with changes in social structure in certain matrilineal groups in North America. The historical setting was contact with white society and the disruption to native societies this caused. The terminological change was seen as proceeding from 'Crow' to generational, and was relatively unproblematic in itself, owing to documentary evidence taken from dictionaries compiled by missionaries 200 to 300 years earlier. The social structural aspects were harder to determine and therefore more controversial. Rather more strikingly, a long article published by Fêng Han-yi in 1937 traced changes in the Chinese kinship terminology over a period of more than 2000 years. The main evidence here was manuals of mourning grades, one of which, the Êrh Ya, was datable to about 200 BC. This evidence indicates that the Chinese terminology was a symmetric prescriptive one at this period, though today it is completely non-prescriptive. Such evidence is rarely available, however, and even where it is, it need not show change at all: the Japanese terminology, for example, has been remarkably stable over the 1100 years since it was first recorded (Smith 1962).

But there are other methods of tackling the question of change in terminologies, though they cannot with safety be applied to social structure – indeed, these methods necessarily stress the linguistic aspect of kinship terminology. The major one here is the ordinary method of historical linguistics, in which lexical items in related languages are compared to trace changes in their meaning; but sometimes evidence of linguistic change internal to a language may be available. Examples here include the work of N. J. Allen (for example, 1976), Robert Blust (1980), Isidore Dyen and David Aberle (1974), Steven Tyler (1984) and Gregory Forth (see below); the same basic assumptions are present elsewhere, for example, with Thomas Trautmann (1981), and in Needham's work on Sumba (1980), even though there are no actual linguistic reconstructions. In Needham's case, these are now being supplied in a series of articles by Forth (for example, 1990), looking at the question of historical proof specifically. The chief problem with such work is that although it can reconstruct lexical items, through comparative phonology, it is much more difficult to reconstruct meanings. One may, for example, be able to reconstruct the original term in the proto-language from which those now meaning MB in the daughter languages have derived, but what guarantee is there that the original meaning was the same?

Other attempts to trace changes in terminological patterns have been based more on logical than on lexical comparisons, particularly on the internal economy and coherence of some patterns in relation to others. Work here falls into two groups, which seem to have produced very similar results independently and to a large extent in relative ignorance of one another. In America, two pioneers were Gertrude Dole (1957) and Elman Service (1960). In Britain, Needham's work led to similar conclusions, which have been equally influential with some, but have also generated considerable scepticism, especially from those hostile to either structuralist or evolutionist approaches or both.

The recognition of typologies of terminological patterns, if not of complete terminologies, is an integral part of such work, though they are not in themselves new. Previous instances are those of Lowie (1928) and Murdock (1949), the former using descriptive labels and the pattern of the $+1$ level, the latter those of sample societies and the pattern of ego's level. Many feel the latter sorts of designation to beg all sorts of undesirable questions and hence prefer to avoid them (they are discussed more fully in chapter 5, above). Both sorts are based on actual equations and distinctions between specifications, rather than on properties such as age and generation, as in Kroeber and Goodenough. As such, they provide a link between the cruder typologies of Morgan and the more complete picture provided by Needham.

Needham's typology (for example, 1971), though not free from all objection, is perhaps on the whole the most satisfactory. He prefers different labels for both terminological patterns and the equations and distinctions from which they derive their character. Thus a prescriptive equation is one which unites a consanguineal cross relative with an affinal one, such as MB = WF, and the same description can be applied to the whole terminology if appropriate. A two-line or symmetric prescriptive terminology is one that 'sorts jural statuses into two lines', of which the equation $F = FB \neq MB = FZH$ is representative (a 'Dravidian' equation); a three-line or asymmetric prescriptive terminology would split the last equation, so that $F = FB \neq MB \neq FZH$ – that is, wife-givers $\neq$ wife-takers $\neq$

parallel relatives (a 'Kachin' equation). This use of the term 'line' is apt to be confusing, because it suggests the image of a descent line and therefore even of a descent group, despite the fact that societies with such terminological equations need not have such groups, or need not use them in actual alliances. It is not actually Needham's innovation, but is found in the work of Radcliffe-Brown, Reo Fortune, Lloyd Warner, Leach and others. A further source of potential confusion is that Needham regularly talks of lineal equations as those that merge collaterals with lineal kin – for example, F = FB – which conflicts with Lowie's better-established and completely contrary usage, which is not itself actually very logical. Needham improved on Lowie's typology by taking full account of the position of the affines of consanguines (for example, FZH) within terminologies, which Lowie had neglected. To round off the picture, although Needham did recognize generational equations, he did not focus on such terminologies in his own work, nor on what he called 'cognatic' or 'non-prescriptive' terminologies, those such as our own, which Lowie had called 'lineal', nor on 'Crow-Omaha' terminologies. Needham's complete rejection of the latter as a separate class (1971: 14–17) is well known, but has not generally been followed. However, like prescriptive terminologies, which they are not, they fall into the class of lineal terminologies, because of the vertical equations they make.

The reason for Lowie's neglect of three-line prescriptive terminologies was probably that in the late 1920s, when he published this typology, such terminologies and the societies associated with them had still not found a secure place in anthropological theory. In the early days of anthropology, 'cross-cousin marriage' mainly meant bilateral exchange. Work on asymmetric systems had long been under way, but mostly by Dutch scholars who, at that time, were much more inclined to write only in their own language. In fact, it was only in the 1950s to 1960s, following the publication of *Elementary Structures*, of Leach's work on the Kachin (1954, 1961) and of Needham's early studies on the Purum (1958a, 1962a: chapter 4) and Lamet (1960a) that such work really became theoretically important in anthropology. This, in its turn, was because they were far more localized than other terminological systems, being found mainly in parts of eastern Indonesia and South-east Asia – areas dominated colonially and anthropologically by the Dutch and the French respectively, and in which few if any American or English anthropologists had by then worked. Their obscurity persisted longest in the United States, being one probable reason for Needham's difficulties with his American colleagues over prescriptive alliance (his main theoretical interest was on asymmetric systems; *see* 1971, 'Introduction', for his own account of these controversies). Two-line terminologies, on the other hand, were found much more widely, not only in these two areas but also in Australia, South Asia, parts of Oceania, and South America, areas to which British and American anthropologists had much more direct access. Much the same is true of Crow-Omaha (in North America and Africa) and generational (or Hawaiian) terminologies (examples in South-east Asia, Oceania, South America, and so on). Both these latter sorts of system had already been fully accepted by the 1950s, though there was still much dispute about their exact interpretation.

In fact, one of the most widespread terminologies in a global sense would seem to be two-line symmetric ones, which occur in such widely separated parts of the world that they cannot themselves be the result of either historical convergence or diffusion. This is one factor in the belief of Dole, Service, Needham, and others, that such terminologies are historically prior to all other attested ones. Another important factor is that in studies carried out so far, it has not proved possible to derive such terminologies from any other type – indeed, the balance of evidence points to the reverse. For example, in addition to the documentary evidence in Fêng Han-yi (1937) and Benedict (1942) on Chinese, and of Melford Spiro (1977) on Burmese, there is Needham's work (1980) on Sumba, an eastern Indonesian island with a number of related languages and dialects. Here, there are a number of different combinations of terminology and alliance system, namely symmetric alliance with a symmetric terminology, asymmetric alliance with a symmetric terminology, and asymmetric alliance with an asymmetric terminology. However, there are no examples of an asymmetric terminology accompanying a symmetric pattern of affinal alliance, this being another key finding of Needham's work. This conveys a picture of a symmetric ideology of alliance gradually changing into an asymmetric one, with the terminology adjusting, only more slowly. This is no doubt a simplification of the facts as far as actual patterns of alliances are concerned, but these may be subject to a conscious manipulation of the rules. The use of terminology, being an aspect of language, is less conscious and cannot be manipulated so readily, at least in reference. Moreover, changes in it, as in language generally, are unlikely to be reversed. It may also be suggested that terminological changes are harder to effect and therefore more likely to remain in place once made.

The transition on Sumba has been between two sorts of prescriptive terminology, but it is possible to envisage changes into non-prescriptive terminologies also. One such change would involve increasing the distinctions made by the terminology, so that all possible specifications, consanguineal and affinal, were identified (for example, North Indian; Parkin 1990b). From here, a different set of equations might be developed, producing a cognatic terminology: the transition from Latin to its daughter languages is one example (Allen 1989). Another would involve suppressing distinctions, so that only one term were found in each generation (for example, generational; this is contrary to Morgan, who saw this type as prior in the evolutionary sense). This would be an exception to the normal assumption against the evolutionary reduction of terminological distinctions. A third would involve the development of intergenerational equations, not only as in Crow-Omaha, but also as in such prescriptive three-line terminologies as that of the Kachin, which have them on both sides, though never right down the descent line. For some terminologies, of course, there has been little or no change, even in terms of the model – we still have many examples of the type that is supposedly the most fundamental, that is, symmetric or two-line prescriptive (for example, the Kariera in Australia).

Perhaps the single most important distinction among terminological types, however, is the dichotomy between those that distinguish cross from parallel relatives and those that do not. Such distinctions are often found even where prescriptive and classificatory equations are lacking, and it is in this respect, of course, that terminologies and alliance systems may most obviously resemble one another – parallel relatives may be in the same exogamous group and are often assimilated to siblings, and so are usually excluded from marriage, whereas cross relatives are typically alliance partners in scores of societies. This is also fundamental from the point of view of the ideology of exchange and continuing alliance. Repeated parallel-cousin marriage, by contrast, limits exchange and is generally associated with the endogamy and separation of a class or clan within the society. The purest and most economical terminological expression of this distinction is to be found in two-line symmetric prescriptive terminologies: three-line ones keep the distinction between cross and parallel relatives but make other distinctions (for example, primary wife-takers and wife-givers) within the former group (for example, FZH ≠ MB). This in itself is an additional reason for seeing two-line terminologies as more fundamental.

One feature often, though not invariably, found in two-line terminologies is equations between members of alternate generations, especially between ego's and either +2 or −2 or both; or between +2 and −2 alone. Examples are to be found in Australia, South America and middle India. The feature has puzzled many anthropologists, Aberle (1967) calling it 'a finding in search of a theory'. However, Allen (1986) has suggested that by exploiting both this principle and the cross-parallel distinction to the limit, one would arrive at a still simpler terminology, one in which only two terminological levels were distinguished, that of ego's, terminologically identical with the +2 and −2 levels, and that of the levels adjacent to ego, terminologically identical with one another but not with ego's. Given also a gender distinction (probably a relative one), only four terms would be needed – hence the term 'tetradic' for the hypothetical society with this pattern. A well-known terminology that represents a close approximation to this model is that of the Kariera in Australia (Dumont 1983: chapter 5). Some Dravidian terminologies of central India have a similar basic pattern (Trautmann 1981; Parkin 1992), and the fact that their linguistic relatives further south lack alternate-generation equations suggests a historical sequence of some sort – most probably away from such equations, which seem to be the least stable under conditions of change. No known terminology, however, is fully tetradic in the sense described.

Despite the documentary evidence of a few cases, such historically focused work still needs to develop adequate defences against its sceptics. The typologies used are based on ideal types, and it is very rare to find actual terminologies corresponding to them in every detail. This objection, however, can often be circumvented by applying them to particular levels or lines separately. In practice, for example, it is often ego's level or line that stands out as being different, those on either side of it being more in agreement with one another. Thus in India many Munda terminologies are generational in ego's level but two-line prescriptive (with the corollary that affinal terms are normally separate) in +1 and −1 (Parkin 1992: chapter 7). Similarly, most Crow-Omaha terminologies have vertical equations in the exterior lines but not in ego's (though there are exceptions, such as the Gurage of East Africa; Needham 1969). Certainly such work has so far managed to avoid the abstraction of formal analysis in the work of Goodenough, Lounsbury, Scheffler and others, and it stands in complete contrast to the disregard in the latter school of the circumstances in which the terminology has come to assume its present form. A charge that can be directed at both approaches is remoteness from the social context also. However, while for Scheffler and others, it is a matter of principle to define this context very narrowly, for the more historically minded it is mainly a matter of practicability while conducting analyses rather than of irreducible principle. Few are prepared to give up the hope that a clearer idea of the connection between terminology and social structure will one day emerge, but at the same time there is an eagerness to avoid the mistakes of earlier examples of evolutionism. This implies a stricter conceptual separation of the two aspects, even in work which seeks eventually to connect them, taking to heart, at least as a matter of prudence, Kroeber's dictum (1909) that 'the burden of proof must be entirely with the propounder of such views'. In stressing the linguistic aspect of terminology, it is also returning to Kroeber's position, though it is less sceptical than he was that typologies cannot be constructed from principles of terminological organization.

1 5

Ethnographic Examples anc
Further Reading

In this chapter, some ethnographic examples are offered of the major concepts discussed in this book, and suggestions for further reading given on a chapter by chapter basis.

Part I

1 Introductory

One recent work claiming to provide a scientific approach to kinship is Hughes 1988, which specifically attacks conventional anthropological approaches from a sociobiological point of view. For an equally trenchant defence of the anthropological position, *see* Sahlins 1977. An example of a basically psychological explanation for the social facts of kinship is Homans and Schneider 1955, criticized by Needham 1962a. Within anthropology, Radcliffe-Brown was perhaps the most dedicated proponent of the now unpopular view that the discipline should develop as a natural science (e.g. 1952: chapters 9, 10). On abbreviations and symbols, *see* Barnard and Good 1984: chapter 1.

2 Descent (see *Figs 2.1–2.3*)

The Juang are an ethnic group in central India (northern Orissa) of about 20,000 people, studied by McDougal (1964; *see also* Parkin

1992: 168–73). Their descent system is patrilineal, and divided into three levels of segmentation. The first consists of 18 patriclans or *bok*, which are totemic and exogamous, dispersed in several villages, and have no property in common. They are divided into 38 local descent groups, which are unnamed but generally unique to a village; they are the basic units in spouse exchange. The third level are the lineages or *kutumali*, two or three to a village, usually three generations in depth. They are the preferred units in inheritance (i.e. if there are no sons who can be direct heirs); they contribute to the brideprices of their members and distribute incoming brideprices among themselves; and they have some ritual identity as units. Genealogical connections are traced only within local descent groups and lineages. Clans are identifiable only through totems. When marriages are being discussed, the totems of the partners are compared; only if they are different may the marriage take place. All levels of segmentation are exogamous. Residence is virilocal.

The descent system of certain subgroups of Khasi of north-east India forms a complete contrast in basic respects to the Juang (*see* Nakane 1967). The Khasi are divided into matrilineal clans, called *kur*, and residence is uxorilocal. Families are also matrilineal, i.e. they are formed around brother-sister, not husband-wife pairs, and contain only the children of the sister, not the brother. The latter's wife and children live elsewhere, and he joins them overnight, spending his days at his sister's home. Similarly, the sister's husband comes to spend each night with her in house.

An example of a cognatic descent system are the Maori, studied by Firth (1957). The unit of descent here is the *hapu*, which is from eight to ten generations deep, non-unilineal, with a common name and common set of ancestors. Membership in it may be claimed through either male or female links. Residence is also important, provided some kin ties can also be demonstrated. An individual may belong to several groups. Marriage, however, takes place for preference within the *hapu* (i.e. the *hapu* is preferentially endogamous), in which case the children are members of it through both parents. This in its turn affects their ability to trace links and therefore claim membership in more than one group (i.e. here endogamy conflicts with choice of membership).

Another example is the descent system on Mafia Island, Tanzania, studied by Patricia Caplan (1969). Here, there are six cognatic descent groups, called *vikao* (singular *kikao*), each consisting of between 60 and 200 members. Membership can be claimed through either male or female links. Genealogies are kept, often ten generations deep, for descent is more important than residence. Nonetheless, each *kikao* resides together under the authority of an elder, has a name and farmland in common, and some ritual unity.

Vikao are segmented into *matumbo* (singular *tumbo*), each under a lesser elder, and occasionally segments become new *vikao*. There is no rule of exogamy or endogamy, though Caplan found that statistically, 60 per cent of all first marriages took place within the *kikao*. There were many divorces, however, and second marriages were usually conducted outside it. Forty-five per cent of the population were members of only one *vikao*, 55 per cent of more than one. There was no particular rule of residence: individuals lived wherever they had close ties of descent, whether through their fathers or mothers.

Thus residence with and claims within particular *vikao* are a matter of choice. On what is this choice based? First, there is the question of land, which is divided into two types, wet land and bushland. Wet land is irrigated, easy to work, and workable throughout the year, but suitable only for rice and sweet potatoes. Bushland is poorer and harder to work, but it is possible to grow other crops on it, such as cereals, beans, millet and gourd. Thus both sorts of land have their advantages, but any one *kikao* or *tumbo* may have only one type: the desire to grow a certain crop may therefore influence the claims one makes to membership of a particular group. The second factor is that five of the six *vikao* have claims to power over local mosques, which brings prestige, though not to an equal extent. The sixth *kikao* has no mosque, though it does have a lot of land. Thus although *vikao* are ranked, status does not correspond with amount of land. The higher ranking *vikao* also tend to be the most endogamous, presumably because of the prestige with which they are associated and the desire to retain it through endogamy.

For an example of double unilineal descent, we may return to

India. The Kondaiyankottai Maravar, a subcaste of Tamil Nadu (Good 1991: 76–8), have patrilineal *kottu*, which are exogamous and localized, control inheritance and succession, and are the units within which family deities are transmitted from generation to generation. More important for the regulation of marriage, however, are the matrilineal *kilai*, which are not localized, and membership of which receives greater emphasis. Marriage therefore has to take both sorts of descent group into account.

Needham (1971: 11) offers the Penan of Borneo as an example of the necessity of distinguishing descent from inheritance, succession and residence. Here, while descent in the sense of recruitment to groups is cognatic, names devolve patrilineally, other inheritance is unilineal in both modes (i.e. double unilineal, depending on what is transmitted) and residence uxorilocal (i.e. with wife's parents). Another example is north India, a region overwhelmingly with patrilineal descent and virilocal residence, but where again inheritance may be unilineal in both modes: while immovables and most movables are almost invariably inherited patrilineally, female clothes and ornaments may be inherited matrilineally, sometimes pre-mortem (e.g. with dowry at marriage; *see* Goody 1990).

For further discussion of unilineal descent and descent groups, *see* Radcliffe-Brown 1950, Fortes 1953, Sahlins 1961, J. A. Barnes 1961, Holy 1979; Kuper 1982 (the latter a particularly sceptical view); it is unfortunate that Dumont's excellent account (1971: Part 2) has not been published in English translation. On cognatic (or bilateral) systems, in addition to Firth and Caplan, there are Freeman 1958, Davenport 1959 and Murdock 1960. On complementary filiation, *see* Fortes 1953, 1959. On double unilineal descent, *see* Goody 1961, Forde 1950. Further on the desirability of distinguishing descent from inheritance, succession and residence, *see* Rivers 1914: 85–8.

3 The family and other kin groupings

The Iban of Borneo (Freeman 1958) provide an example of an extended family. The society is divided residentially into longhouses, each containing about 200 people and 35 families. Each longhouse has an open veranda (*tanju*) running the whole length of the longhouse, backed by an internal corridor (*ruwai*). The longhouse is divided crosswise into *bilek*, or private rooms for each family.

The longhouse forms a ritual unit, with a chief (*tuai rumah*), but has no common property or land. Each *bilek* contains either a nuclear family or a family three, occasionally four, generations deep. Families are often, but not necessarily, linked to one another through bilateral links. Each *bilek* lives, eats and works together, holding farming land, canoes, ritual objects and ancestral property such as gongs, clothes, jewellery, Chinese pots and Malay cannon (some of the latter are used as brideprice) in common. The *bilek* is also exogamous, membership of it being through birth, in-marriage or adoption. Residence is also described as utrolocal, i.e. residence in the *bilek* depends on links to either mother or father, but simultaneous membership in more than one *bilek* is not allowed. Transferring residence on marriage means ending claims to membership in the *bilek* of birth; one must bring one's share of one's ancestral property with one on transfer. Inheritance depends on residence. Children have equal rights to inherit regardless of gender, but there is a restriction in that only one child inherits the *bilek*: other children must found or join another *bilek*. *Bilek* often split up as a result of quarrels or when one member wants to take his or her share of the ancestral property. Indivisible property, such as the sacred rice and the wetstone, both of which have ritual significance, must remain with the original *bilek*.

In addition to the *bilek*, the Iban also have the *bejalai* or kindred (*see* Fig. 3.2), formed around one person as leader, often a ritual expert, for expeditions to collect forest produce or to trade (farming, by contrast, is a *bilek* affair). In the past, the *bejalai* was also significant in providing support in warfare. Each *bejalai* is named after its leader and links between five and 50 cognatically related people, though each individual belongs potentially to more than one.

For further reading, *see* Kapadia 1955: chapter 10; Parry 1979: chapter 6, on the Hindu (and patrilineal) joint family. Historically, the Nayar of south India provided a dramatic example of a matrilineal joint family (Fuller 1976); more generally on this type, *see*

Schneider and Gough 1961. On the matrifocal family, *see* Smith 1973. On residence and family types, *see* Barnard and Good 1984: 78–84; on the terms 'virilocal, uxorilocal', Adam 1948. The Trobriand Islanders provide the standard example of avunculocal residence (Malinowski 1929). Freeman 1961 is the standard theoretical work on the kindred.

4 Marriage

On marriage generally, *see* Mair 1971. McLennan (1865) coined the term 'exogamy', which Lévi-Strauss (1949) later combined with incest and exchange to produce a whole theory of marriage as alliance (*see* above, chapters 12, 13). On the difficulties of defining marriage, *see* Leach 1961: chapter 4; Riviere 1971. On the woman-woman marriages of the Nuer, *see* Evans-Pritchard 1951: 108–9. Bridewealth and dowry are compared in Goody and Tambiah 1973, Goody 1976, 1990. Also on marriage prestations, *see* Comaroff 1980, on bridewealth and brideprice, Evans-Pritchard 1931. Parkin 1990a compares hypergamy and hypogamy. On polyandry, *see* Prince Peter 1963, on levirate, Evans-Pritchard 1951: 112–15, on widow inheritance and sororate, Parkin 1992: chapter 6. H. T. Fischer's term 'polykoity' is discussed in Leach 1961: 105–6.

5 Kinship (relationship) terminology

See especially above, chapter 12; also Parkin 1996, on genealogy and category. On preference, prescription, practice and the relationship between different levels of analysis, *see* Needham 1973, Good 1981 (a south Indian example discussed below), both partly responses to Schneider 1962. Radcliffe-Brown's views on terminology are set out in 1952: chapter 13. On typologies, *see* Barnard and Good 1984: 60–5. The first typology in chapter 5 above ('generational' etc.) is associated with Lowie (1928), the second ('Hawaiian' etc.) with Murdock (1949). Lounsbury (1968) first established the 'Iroquois' pattern as different from 'Dravidian' (on the latter, *see also* Trautmann 1981). The typology utilizing lines is Needham's (e.g. 1971: 13–24).

6 Symmetric affinal alliance [see Figs 6.1–6.1(c)]

The work of Lévi-Strauss on kinship systems (1969, originally 1949) is a crucial text for this and the next chapter, and is clearly summarized in French by Dumont (1971: Part 3). Fortune (1933) groups together the three basic prescriptive models in a very brief article. *See also* Maybury-Lewis 1965.

One standard example of a symmetric system is the Kariera of Australia (Dumont 1983: 175–91, 201–3), who are divided into four sections grouped into two generations, as below:

generation A: Burung   Banaka
generation B: Karimera Palyeri

Intermarriage takes place between individuals who are classed as bilateral cross cousins to one another, and between the two sections in each generation: i.e. members of Burung intermarry only with Banaka, the children of such marriages being in either Karimera or Palyeri, according to the respective groups of their parents, and vice versa. Thus, each section unites people of alternate genealogical levels (in opposition to members of adjacent levels) and common descent (in opposition to affines).

The Cashinahua of south-east Peru (Kensinger 1984) are divided into four marriage sections, which are grouped into two patrimoieties, as below:

moiety: Inubakebu   Duainubakebu
sections: Awainubakebu   Yawainubakebu
           Kanainubakebu Dunuinubakebu

The sections are also namesake groups: ego shares names with his or her same-sex PP and CC. The preference is for moiety exogamy and marriage with bilateral cross cousins: sections Awainubakebu and Yawainubakebu intermarry, their children being in Kanainubakebu or Dunuinubakebu; and vice versa. In a sample of 91 marriages, it was found that while 71 obeyed the rules, there were four marriages into the right moiety but the wrong section and a further 11 at into the wrong moiety. Wrong marriages are tolerated, though subject to supernatural sanctions, witchcraft accusations etc. Although such cases represent a confusion of categories, they are reckoned to be better than remaining unmarried (they may reflect demographic difficulties in everyone marrying according to the rules). The moiety or section membership of the woman, but not the man, is altered. Marriages (for a male) with actual M, FZ, MM, FM, Z, D, ZD and CD are regarded as incestuous (*chakahaida*) and would not be allowed: none was recorded. Despite the presence of patrimoieties, residence is uxorilocal.

Another South American group with a broadly similar rule of marriage is the Piaroa of the Venezuela-Guyana border (Overing 1975). Although patriclans and moieties exist, however, they are of only cosmological significance and are not concerned with the regulation of marriage. The society is also divided into preferentially endogamous bilateral descent groups centred on a communal house, called *itso'de*, with up to about 60 members. Marriage is preferred not only within the *itso'de* but also to close relatives: while having affines is regarded as essential, they are also potentially a source of ritual danger. It is therefore better if they are also close kin within the *itso'de* – they tend to be assimilated to consanguines in later generations – and marriage to actual cross cousins (*chirekwa/-o*) is preferred. Unreciprocated exchange is also dangerous; hence there is also a preference for direct, simultaneous exchange between men who are related as male cross cousins. If other sorts of marriage occur, the partners and most of their immediate relatives are reclassified according to the kin terms that would be used if the marriage had conformed to the above preference: for example, although marriages occasionally occur between *chiminya* (MB) and *chuhörihu* (ZD), they thereafter become *chirekwa/-o* (bilateral cross cousins) to one another.

Good has used his data on the Kondaiyankottai Maravar of Tamil Nadu, south India (1981), specifically to illustrate the level of coherence between terminology, rules and behaviour in such systems. All members of this subcaste are regarded as kin and are normally addressed with kin terms. The matrilineal *kilai* (*see* above) is more strictly exogamous than the patrilineal *kottu*, with which people are generally less familiar. The terminology is basically two-line prescriptive, though with additional categories to express relative age. The prescribed spouse for a man is a *kolundiyal*, which includes junior female bilateral cross cousins, and for a woman an *attan*, which includes senior male bilateral cross cousins. The preference, however, is for marriages between FZDy and MBSe, i.e. for a close relative (there is also a vague preference for village endogamy), and for the woman to be younger than the man. The preference for marriages with close relatives is justified on the grounds that the character, wealth and standing of the spouses are already known to their prospective affines and that the amount of prestations required to be exchanged will be less. Direct exchange is allowed, i.e. despite the preference, both types of cross cousin may be married, unlike the situation with asymmetric prescriptive alliance. It is often said, however, that if one of the exchange marriages were to break down for any reason, the other would do so too. Polygyny and divorce are allowed.

As regards behaviour, Good's samples showed that with genealogical cross cousins, there was an almost equal preference for MBDy and FZDy, in the range of 8–12 per cent each: this represents a total figure of about 25 per cent of marriages to first cross cousins, a comparatively high proportion for such systems. This still means that most marriages are not with the genealogical cross cousin but with a member of the same category. These data also indicate that the declared preference for one sort of cross cousin over the other is not actually followed as regards genealogical cross cousins. In 59 per cent of marriages, however, male ego's wife came from his father's *kilai*, making these marriages formally equivalent to FZD marriages. As for exogamous rules, both *kilai* and *kottu* exogamy were obeyed to a very high degree, as was the relative age requirement. These rules seem actually to have been obeyed more than the marriage prescription, and there was less sensitivity surrounding breaches of the latter than breaches of the rules of exogamy. Nonetheless, 95 per cent of marriages obeyed the terminological prescription.

The Aranda of Australia are the standard example of an eight-section system, i.e. of marriage to spouses defined minimally as second cross cousins [Korn 1973; *see* above, Figs. 6.2–6.2(a)]. They are divided into several patriclans, and residence is patrilocal. There are two patrimoieties, labelled with the absolute names of Alurinja and Kwatjarinja. There are also several relative labels: for example, for any ego, one's own moiety is *nakarakia* (roughly, 'our fathers'), the opposite one *etnakarakia* (roughly, 'their fathers'). There are also eight marriage sections. Marriage for either male or female ego is prescribed to someone in the category *noa* (FMBSD/FFZSD/ MMBDD/MFZDD and FMBSS/FFZSS/MMBDS/MFZDS). That the sections are not required is shown by two other Australian groups, the Mara and the Dieri, who lack them though having the same marriage rules (in addition, the clans and moieties of the Dieri are matrilineal).

Further on symmetric systems, both two- and four-line, Korn 1973 and Dumont 1983: chapters 5, 6, discuss Australian systems (Dumont challenges double descent theory as an explanation for such systems); also Needham 1962b. On south and central India, *see* Dumont 1953, 1983: chapters 1, 2; Trautmann 1981; on Sri Lanka, Yalman 1962. Further lowland South American examples appear in Kensinger (ed.) 1985.

7 Asymmetric affinal alliance (see Figs 7.1–7.3)

The affinal alliance system of Mamboru, a domain on north-west Sumba, Indonesia, is described by Needham (1987). There is a distinction between wife-givers (*yera*, literally WB) and wife-takers (*layia*, literally ZH), the former being superior in status. Marriage is preferred to the genealogical cross cousin (matrilateral for male ego, patrilateral for female ego). Marriage circles consisting of the theoretical minimum of three groups are seen as ideal, and this is expressed in the terminological equation of MBW and FZHZ; similarly, marriages to WBW are prohibited because, with just three alliance groups, she would fall into the normally prohibited category FZD. The fact that there are no separate terms for wife-givers' wife-givers or wife-takers' wife-takers (cf. Kachin, below) also expresses this ideal. There is generational continuity of alliances between local descent groups or *uma*, which are grouped into *kabisu*, the latter being dispersed in many villages. Residence is normally virilocal: only poor men who cannot afford a brideprice marry uxorilocally (perhaps to serve WF as heir, if the latter has no son). There are many such systems in eastern Indonesia, a further one being described by R. H. Barnes (domain of Kédang, 1974).

One of the earliest examples of this system to be described was the Kachin, of Upper Burma (Leach 1945). They are divided into seven or eight patriclans or *amyu*, which are not necessarily exogamous but are themselves divided further into *htinggaw*. Leach calls the latter 'local descent groups', which are more strictly exogamous. As regards the affinal alliance system, four groups can be identified from the perspective of any ego: one's own (*kahpu-kanan ni*), who are basically one's agnates; wife-givers (*mayu ni*), who are superior in status; wife-takers (*dama ni*), who are inferior in status); and *lawu-lahta ni*, or those not visibly related to one's own group by either descent or (at least, for the time being) by affinal alliance. One's *mayu* and *dama* should always be different, and their difference in status is conceived of in all sorts of ritual ways: for example, auspicious spirits are defined as *mayu*, inauspicious as *dama*. There are usually many more groups than the minimum of three involved in any circle of alliances, and the circles intersect freely; however, there is usually continuity of alliances over generations. A male ego marries a *nam* (not actual MyBD, but someone classed with her), a female ego a *gu* (not actual FeZS, but someone classed with him). FZD-MBS marriage is banned as incestuous, though these categories are not equated with siblings terminologically, as they are in some such systems. The terminology can be interpreted as identifying five alliance groups (i.e. including wife-givers' wife-givers and wife-takers' wife-takers; cf. Mamboru, above). It is also skewed, in the sense that the status difference between *mayu* and *dama* is reflected in the distribution of terms between different genealogical levels: e.g. *nam* also occurs in junior levels, *gu* also in senior levels.

The kinship terminology of the Lamet, a group in neighbouring Laos with a similar system, is also skewed (Izikowitz 1951). This group of about 6,000 people living in about 100 villages is divided into seven totemic, exogamous clans called *ta* (literally 'ancestor, grandfather'); each village has members of more than one clan. There is some direct exchange between clans, but the spouse-exchange units are the local lineages into which the clans are divided, exchange being asymmetric between any two. The prescribed term for men and women is *haem* (MBDms and FZSws). Bridewealth consists typically of two to four buffaloes or pigs, gongs and a bronze drum, and there is usually a period of brideservice. Counter-prestations going along with the wife are typically a silk shirt, wine jug, Chinese bowl, axe, chopping knife, lance, turban, cotton skirts and silver bracelets. Though superior, wife-givers owe wife-takers ritual services: it is their ancestral spirits who enable children to be produced.

8 FZD and ZD marriage (see Figs 8.1, 8,2)

Claimed examples of FZD marriage include the Siane of the New Guinea Highlands (Salisbury 1956) and the Pende of Kasai Province, Zaire (de Souseberge 1955). Among the former, there is a preference for FZD as a spouse, with an ideology of overall reciprocity between clans. In only 23 per cent of a sample, however, did wives come from the clan of FZH (i.e. there were even fewer marriages with FZD herself). Also, there are no lasting structural ties between clans but, instead, a tendency towards the almost simultaneous exchange of lineage sisters. The term for cross cousin, *hovofaro*, does not distinguish between the two types of cross cousin. The Pende have matrilineal endogamous clans (*iputa*), divided into exogamous *mavumo* (literally 'stomach'), though the actual exchange units appear to be the *majigo* (literally 'hearth, home, family'), though they are sometimes four generations deep. There is a preference for FZD and a ban on MBD, reflected in the composition of the kin term *gisoni* FZDms, MBSws, though the rest of the terminology is non-prescriptive. There are some vertical equations, such as MBDms = D, FZSws = F, typical 'Crow' equations. On the plausibility of FZD marriage as a system, *see* Needham 1958b, 1960b (a sceptical position).

The Trio of the Brazil-Surinam border provide an example of regular ZD marriage, though it is not the only form of marriage. Marriages take place between *emerimpe*, literally cross cousins and sisters' daughters, though the term is actually applied to anyone considered unrelated (Riviere 1969). Potential wives, however, are often described as daughters of *nosi* (FZ but also PM) or *ti* (MB), with a slight preference for the former. In a sample, about a half of all marriages conformed to this bilateral rule, a figure which rises to 80 per cent if marriages to ZD (apparently eZD for preference) are included. Some marriages take place with the genealogical ZD, but most Trio marriages partners are not traceable genealogically. Descent is cognatic, and there is also the strong inside-outside dichotomy found in the Amazon Basin – the outside being considered potentially dangerous: ZD marriage is connected with avoiding this danger. For more on ZD marriage, *see* Lave 1966, Riviere 1966, Good 1980.

9 Non-prescriptive quasi-systems (see Figs 9.1, 9.2, 9.3)

Given the controversy surrounding the status of Crow-Omaha systems mentioned in chapter 9, finding unambiguous examples of them is not an entirely straightforward matter. One modern description of an 'Omaha' system is Bowden's (1983) of the Kwoma of the Sepik area of Papua New Guinea. They have patrilineal clans, their terminology has extensive vertical equations of 'Omaha' type, they lack positive marriage rules, and they do not allow marriages between the same descent lines to be repeated in the following three generations. The latter rule is framed as a series of prohibitions on taking women from particular descent lines (though not the wider clans). Among descent lines prohibited as a source of spouses for a male ego are those of WB, BWB, MB, FMB, and FFMB, while specific kin types forbidden him include ZHZ, FZHZ, ZD, FZD, ZSD, ZSSD, ZSSSD, FZSD, FZSSD, FZSSSD. Alliance relationships, once created, are continued into the following generation and possibly for two further generations, but they are maintained through the exchange of gifts and services (political, ritual etc.), not of women. As those involved in the initial exchanges die off, they are replaced by their direct patrilineal descendants as long as the principals to the marriage survive. Bowden shows that it is these original exchangers and their descendants who tend to be classified together through vertical terminological equations.

That this classification does not invariably occur with such rules dispersing alliance can be seen if we return to the Juang (McDougal 1963; also Parkin 1992: 168–73). Although McDougal does not give a list of prohibited descent lines or kin groups of the sort that are recorded for the Kwoma, he shows that the Juang have similar rules against the repetition of marriages between any two local descent groups in the following generation, and, according to some of his data, in the following three. However, the Juang terminology is totally devoid of any 'Omaha' equations (although it is two-line prescriptive in its treatment of consanguines, it has no cognate-affine equations). Conversely, the terminology of the Purum, on the Indo-Burma border, has a number of such equations, though it is basically a skewed three-line prescriptive terminology like those of the Kachin and Lamet (above). They also resemble the latter is having asymmetric affinal alliance based on marriage into the class that includes MBD (FZS for female ego; *see* Needham 1958a; 1962a: chapter 4).

McKinley (1971a) gives a good account of the various explanations offered for Crow-Omaha systems; his own explanation (1971b) is criticized by R. H. Barnes (1976), following Needham's dismissal of Crow-Omaha terminologies as a separate class (1971: 14–16). Barnes (1984) has also re-examined the actual Omaha ethnography in the light of the questions raised by Crow-Omaha systems. On the notion of semi-complex structures, *see* Lévi-Strauss 1966. The work of Héritier (e.g. 1981) is also significant here.

Recent discussions of patrilateral parallel cousin marriage are Donnan 1988 and Holy 1989. One example of this system comes from the Kurds of northern Iraq (Barth 1954). They are divided into *tira* or lineages, units in feud and landownership, although inheritance of land is retained preferentially within the localized *tira* segment, with brothers being preferred to cousins. FBD marriage is the preferred form; a woman's FBS has the first claim on her, one for which violence is a possible sanction. In such a marriage, the husband's kin are responsible for the wedding expenses, but they do not pay a brideprice. Despite the preference, only about a half of all marriages were between patrilateral parallel cousins; the rest were with MBD, ZD or non-kin. This sort of alliance is less significant in respect of property than in feud. In feud, the support of one's father and brothers can be taken for granted, but that of one's brother's son cannot: by giving him one's daughter in marriage and not demanding a brideprice, his support for life is theoretically acquired. Among Bedouin, there is a similar system, which involves patrilineal, virilocal clan segments (Murphy and Kasdan 1963). Again, a male ego has first claim on his FBD; if he does not have one, he goes to his nearest agnatic cousin. To counteract the tendency for FBD marriage to isolate segments from one another, in southern Tunisia only one brother marries FBD, the rest conducting alliances elsewhere to extend the lineage's ties (Cuisinier 1962).

10 The meaning of kinship

Needham (1971) and Schneider (1984) were among the first to question the usefulness of 'kinship' as an object of anthropological study. The sentiment that kinship is essentially an empty category is found in a different form with Beattie (1964; cf. Schneider 1964). On changes in kinship in the West since late antiquity, see Goody 1983. On Western ideologies of kinship, see Schneider 1968 (on America), Strathern 1992 (on England). On the various forms of pseudo-kinship, see Barnard and Good 1984: 150–4. On the new reproductive technologies, see Riviere 1985. On kinship and contract, see Maine 1861.

The theme of personhood as an aspect of kinship is exemplified by David 1973 and Östör et al. 1982 (both on south Asia). The distinction between inside and outside in place of group formation as informing kinship is especially associated with lowland South America (e.g. Riviere 1969: Part III). The differential combination of male and female aspects within the person is discussed in Strathern 1988, as is the relevance of gender for kinship generally in Papua New Guinea. On gender in this context, see also Goddard 1994. Moore (1964) discusses certain symbolic aspects of descent.

The Basques are an example of an ethnic group with a particularly strong sense of common, age-old descent, based on their claim to be Europe's oldest population and the oldest occupants of the territory on which they live (see MacClancy 1993). Bornemann (1992) deals with the interaction of kinship and identity in the former two Germanies. See also Bestard-Camps (1991) on Catalonian kinship; Astuti 1995 on the Vezo (Madagascar); Raheja and Gold (1994) on north India.

Part II

Key references to theories discussed in chapters 11 to 14 are given in those chapters. The most important books for further general introductory reading, especially of theory, are Barnard and Good 1984 and Dumont 1971 (the latter unfortunately still untranslated). Fox 1967 is now rather old and has been superseded in some respects, but is still useful provided the author's flirtation with biology and ecology in the earlier chapters can be kept in perspective. Schusky 1974 is also useful, and contains further case studies, as does Keesing 1975. Although it discusses anthropologists, Harris 1990 is written more from a sociological perspective and is frankly quite limited for the anthropology student apart from the most general issues. Another old work, Bucher and Selby 1968, is unreliable in many respects. Bohannon and Middleton (eds) 1968a, 1968b are useful collections of certain key texts, though mainly early ones. Service 1985 discusses the main earlier theories of kinship (i.e. up to about the 1960s) in a very approachable fashion.

Bibliography

Included is material referred to in chapters 11 to 15. Recommended books directed particularly at the student are marked with an asterisk.

Aberle, David F., 'A Scale of Alternate Generation Terminology', *Southwestern Journal of Anthropology* 23, 261–78, (1967).

Adam, Leonhard, 'Virilocal' and 'Uxorilocal', *Man* 48, 12, (1948).

Allen, N. J., 'Sherpa Kinship Terminology in Diachronic Perspective', *Man* 11, 569–87, (1976).

— 'Tetradic Theory: An Approach to Kinship', *Journal of the Anthropological Society of Oxford* 17/2, 87–109, (1986).

— 'The Evolution of Kinship Terminologies', *Lingua*, 77, 173–85, (1989).

Astuti, Rita, *People of the Sea: Identity and Descent among the Vezo of Madgascar*, Cambridge, (Cambridge, University Press, 1995).

Bachofen, Johann J., *Das Mutterrecht*, (Stuttgart, Krais und Hoffman, 1861).

*Barnard, Alan and Good, Anthony, *Research Practices in the Study of Kinship*, (London, Academic Press, 1984).

Barnes, J. A., 'African Models in the New Guinea Highlands', *Man* 62, 5–9, (1962).

Barnes, R. H., *Kédang: The Collective Thought of an Eastern Indonesian People*, (Oxford, Clarendon Press, 1974).

— 'Dispersed Alliance and the Prohibition of Marriage: A Reconsideration of McKinley's Explanation of Crow-Omaha Terminologies', *Man* 11, 384–99, (1976).

—*Two Crows Denies It: A History of Controversy in Omaha Sociology*, (Lincoln and London: University of Nebraska Press, 1984).

Barth, Fredrik, 'Father's Brother's Daughter Marriage in Kurdistan', *Southwestern Journal of Anthropology* 10, 164–71, (1954).

Beattie, John, 'Kinship and Social Anthropology', *Man* 64, 101–3, (1964).

Benedict, Paul K., 'Tibetan and Chinese Kinship Terms', *Harvard Journal of Asiatic Studies* 6, 313–37, (1942).

Bestard-Camps, Joan, *What's in a Relative? Household and Family in Formentera*, (New York and Oxford, Berg, 1991).

Blust, Robert, 'Early Austronesian Social Organization: The Evidence of Language', *Current Anthropology* 21/2, 205–47, (1980).

*Bohannan, Paul and Middleton, John (eds), *Kinship and Social Organization*, [New York: The Natural History Press (American Museum Sourcebooks in Anthropology), 1968a].

*—*Marriage, Family and Residence*, [New York: The Natural History Press (American Museum Sourcebooks in Anthropology), 1968b].

Bornemann, John, *Belonging in the two Berlins: Kin, State, Nation*, (Cambridge, Cambridge University Press, 1992).

Bouquet, Mary, 'Family Trees and their Affinities: The Visual Imperative of the Genealogical Diagram', *Journal of the Royal Anthropological Institute* (new series) 2, 43–66, (1996).

Bowden, Ross, 'Kwoma Terminology and Marriage Alliance: The "Omaha" Problem Revisited', *Man* 18, 745–65, (1983).

Caplan, Patricia, 'Cognatic Descent Groups on Mafia Island', *Man* 4, 419–31, (1969).

Comaroff, J. L., *The Meaning of Marriage Payments*, (London, Academic Press, 1980).

Cuisinier, Jean, 'Endogamie et exogamie dans le mariage Arabe', *L'Homme* 2, 80–105, (1962).

Davenport, William, 'Nonunilineal Descent and Descent Groups', *American Anthropologist* 61, 557–72, (1959).

David, Kenneth, 'Till Death do us Part: A Cultural Account of Jaffna Tamil Categories for Kinsmen', *Man* 8/4, 521–35, (1973).

Dole, Gertrude, *The Development of Patterns of Kinship Nomenclature*, (Ann Arbor, University Microfilms, 1957).

Donnan, Hastings, *Marriage among Muslims: Preference and Choice in Northern Pakistan*, (Delhi, Hindustan Publishing Corporation, 1988).

Dumont, Louis, 'The Dravidian Kinship Terminology as an Expression of Marriage', *Man* 53, 34–9, (1953).

*—*Introduction à deux théories d'anthropologie sociale*, (Paris and The Hague, Mouton, 1973).

—*Affinity as a Value: Marriage Alliance in South India, with Comparative Essays on Australia*, (Chicago, University of Chicago Press, 1983).

Durkheim, Emile, *The Division of Labor in Society*, translated by George Simpson, [New York, Free Press, 1964 (1893)].

—*The Elementary Forms of the Religious Life*, translated by J. W. Swain, [London, Allen and Unwin, 1915 (1912)].

Dyen, Isidore and Aberle, David F., *Lexical Reconstruction: The Case of the Proto-Athapaskan Kinship System*, (Cambridge, Cambridge University Press, 1974).

Eggan, Fred, 'Historical Changes in the Choctaw Kinship System', *American Anthropologist* 39, 34–52, (1937).

Engels, Friedrich, *The Origin of the Family, Private Property, and the State*, [New York, International Publishers, 1942 (1884)].

Evans-Pritchard, E. E., 'An Alternative Term for "Bride-price",' *Man* 31, 36–9, (1931).

—*The Nuer*, (Oxford, Clarendon Press, 1940).

—*Kinship and Marriage among the Nuer*, (Oxford, Clarendon Press, 1951).

Fêng Han-yi, 'The Chinese Kinship System', *Harvard Journal of Asiatic Studies* 2, 141 ff., (1937).

Firth, Raymond, 'A Note on Descent Groups in Polynesia', *Man* 57, 4–8, (1957).

—'Bilateral Descent Groups: An Operational Viewpoint', in Isaac Shapera (ed.), *Studies in Kinship and Marriage Dedicated to Brenda Seligman on her 80th Birthday*, (London, Royal Anthropological Institute, 1963).

Fortes, Meyer, *The Dynamics of Clanship Among the Tallensi*, (Oxford, Oxford University Press, 1945).

—*The Web of Kinship Among the Tallensi*, (Oxford, Oxford University Press, 1949).

—'The Structure of Unilineal Descent Groups', *American Anthropologist* 55, 17–41, (1953).

—'Descent, Filiation and Affinity', *Man* 59, 193–7, 206–12, (1959).

Forth, Gregory, 'From Symmetry to Asymmetry: An Evolutionary Interpretation of Eastern Sumbanese Relationship Terminology', *Anthropos* 85/4–6, 373–92, (1990).

Fortune, Reo, 'A Note on Some Forms of Kinship Structure', *Oceania* 4, 1–9, (1993).

*Fox, Robin, *Kinship and Marriage*, (Harmondsworth, Penguin Books, 1967).

Frazer, Sir James, *Totemism and Exogamy* (4 vols), (London, Macmillan, 1910).

Freeman, J. D., 'The Family System of the Iban of Borneo', in Jack Goody (ed.), *The Developmental Cycle in Domestic Groups*, (Cambridge, Cambridge University Press, 1958).

—'On the Concept of the Kindred', *Journal of the Royal Anthropological Institute* 91, 192–220, (1961).

Fuller, C. J., *The Nayars Today*, (Cambridge, Cambridge University Press, (1976).

Fustel de Coulanges, Numa Denis, *The Ancient City*, (New York, Doubleday Anchor, 1864).

Gellner, Ernest, 'Ideal Language and Kinship Structure', *Philosophy of Science* 24, 235–42, (1957).

—'The Concept of Kinship', *Philosophy of Science* 27, 187–204, (1960).

Goddard, Victoria A., 'From the Mediterranean to Europe: Honour, Kinship and Gender', in Victoria A. Goddard, Josep R. Llobera and Cris Shore (eds), *The Anthropology of Europe: Identities and Boundaries in Conflict*, (Oxford, Berg, 1994).

Good, Anthony, 'Elder Sister's Daughter Marriage in South Asia', *Journal of Anthropological Research* 36, 474–500, (1980).

—'Prescription, Preference and Practice: Marriage Patterns Among the Kondaiyankottai Maravar of South India', *Man* 16, 108–29, (1981).

—*The Female Bridegroom: A Comparative Study of Life-Crisis Rituals in South India and Sri Lanka*, (Oxford, Clarendon Press, 1991).

Goodenough, Ward H., 'A Problem in Malayo-Polynesian Social Organization', *American Anthropologist* 57, 71–83, (1954).

—'Componential Analysis and the Study of Meaning', *Language* 32, 195–216, (1956).

Goody, Jack, 'The Mother's Brother and the Sister's Son in West Africa', *Journal of the Royal Anthropological Institute* 89/1, 61–88, (1959).

—'The Classification of Double Descent Systems', *Current Anthropology* 2/1, 3–25, (1961).

—*Production and Reproduction: A Comparative Study of the Domestic Domain*, (Cambridge, Cambridge University Press, 1976).

—*The Development of the Family and Marriage in Europe*, (Cambridge, Cambridge University Press, 1983).

—*The Oriental, the Ancient and the Primitive: Systems of Marriage and the Family in the Pre-industrial Societies of Eurasia*, (Cambridge, Cambridge University Press, 1990).

—(ed.), *The Developmental Cycle in Domestic Groups*, (Cambridge, Cambridge University Press, 1958).

—and Tambiah, Stanley J., *Bridewealth and Dowry*, (Cambridge, Cambridge University Press, 1973).

Hallowell, A. Irving, 'Recent Changes in the Kinship Terminology of the

St. Francis Abenaki', *22nd Proceedings of the International Congress of Americanists* 2, 97–145, (1928).

Harris, C. C., *Kinship*, (Milton Keynes, Open University Press, 1990).

Héritier, Françoise, *L'exercice de la parenté*, (Paris, Gallimard, 1981).

Hocart, A. M., 'Kinship Systems', *Anthropos* 32, 345–51, (1937).

Holy, Ladislav (ed.), *Segmentary Lineage Systems Reconsidered*, [Belfast: The Queens' University (Papers in Social Anthropology, no. 4), 1979].

—*Kinship, Honour and Solidarity: Cousin Marriage in the Middle East*, (Manchester and New York, Manchester University Press, 1989).

Homans, G. C. and Schneider, D. M., *Marriage, Authority and Final Causes: A Study of Unilateral Cross-Cousin Marriage*, (Glencoe, Free Press, 1955).

Izikowitz, Karl Gustav, *Lamet: Hill Peasants in French Indochina*, (Göteborg: Etnografiska Museet, 1951).

Kapadia, K. M., *Marriage and Family in India*, (Calcutta, Oxford University Press, 1955).

Keesing, Roger M., *Kin Groups and Social Structure*, (New York, Holt, Rinehart and Winston, 1975).

Kensinger, Kenneth M., 'An Emic Model of Cashinahua Marriage', in Kensinger (ed.) (1984).

—(ed.), *Marriage Practices in Lowland South America*, (Urbana and Chicago, University of Chicago Press, 1984).

Korn, Francis, *Elementary Structures Reconsidered*, (London, Tavistock, 1973).

Kroeber, Alfred, 'Classificatory Systems of Relationship', *Journal of the Royal Anthropological Institute* 39, 77–84, (1909).

—*Anthropology*, (New York, Brace, Harcourt, 1923).

—*The Nature of Culture*, (Chicago, University of Chicago Press, 1952).

Kuper, Adam, 'Lineage Theory: A Critical Retrospect', *Annual Review of Anthropology* 11, 71–95, (1982).

Lane, Robert B., 'Patrilateral Cross-cousin Marriage: Structural Analysis and Ethnographic Cases', *Ethnology* 1, 467–99, (1962).

Lave, J. C., 'A Formal Analysis of Preferential Marriage with the Sister's Daughter', *Man* 1, 185–200, (1966).

Leach, Sir Edmund, 'Jinghpaw Kinship Terminology', *Journal of the Royal Anthropological Institute* 75, 59–72, (1945).

—'The Structural Implications of Matrilateral Cross-cousin Marriage', *Journal of the Royal Anthropological Institute* 81, 23–53, (1951).

—*Political Systems of Highland Burma*, (London, Athlone Press, 1954).

—'Aspects of Bridewealth and Marriage Stability among the Kachin and Lakher', *Man* 57, 50–5, (1957).

—'Concerning Trobriand Clans and the Kinship Category *tabu'*, in Jack Goody (ed.), *The Developmental Cycle in Domestic Groups*, (Cambridge, Cambridge University Press, 1958).

—'Descent, Filiation and Affinity', *Man* 60, 9–10, (1960).

—*Rethinking Anthropology*, [London, Athlone Press, 1961 (contains Leach 1945, 1951 and 1957)].

—'On Certain Unconsidered Aspects of Double Descent Systems', *Man* 62, 130–4, (1962).

Lévi-Strauss, Claude, 'The Future of Kinship Studies', *Proceedings of the Royal Anthropological Institute* 1965, 13–22, (1966).

—*The Elementary Structures of Kinship*, 2nd edn, translated by Rodney Needham, [London, Eyre and Spottiswoode, 1969 (1949)].

Lounsbury, Floyd, 'A Semantic Analysis of the Pawnee Kinship Usage', *Language* 32, 158–94, (1965).

—'Another View of the Trobriand Kinship Categories', *American Anthropologist* 67/5 (2), 142–85, (1965).

—'The Structural Analysis of Kinship Semantics', in Paul Bohannan and John Middleton (eds), *Kinship and Social Organization*, [New York: The Natural History Press (American Museum Sourcebooks in Anthropology), 1968].

Lowie, Robert, *Primitive Society*, (New York, Horace Liveright, 1920).

—'A Note on Relationship Terminologies', *American Anthropologist* 30, 263–8, (1928).

MacClancy, Jeremy, 'Biological Basques, Sociologically Speaking', in Malcolm Chapman (ed.), *Social and Biological Aspects of Ethnicity*, (Oxford, Oxford University Press, 1993).

McDougal, Charles, *The Social Structure of the Hill Juang*, (Ann Arbor, University Microfilms, 1963).

—'Juang Categories and Joking Relationships', *Southwestern Journal of Anthropology* 20, 319–45, (1964).

McKinley, Robert, 'A Critique of the Reflectionist Theory of Kinship Terminology: The Crow/Omaha Case', *Man* 6/2, 228–47, (1971a).

—'Why do Crow and Omaha Terminologies Exist? A Sociology of Knowledge Interpretation', *Man* 6/3, 408–26, (1971b).

McLennan, John F., *Primitive Marriage*, (Edinburgh, Adam and Charles Black, 1865).

—*Studies in Ancient History*, (London, Macmillan, 1876).

Maine, Sir Henry, *Ancient Law*, (London, John Murray, 1861).

Mair, Lucy, *Marriage*, (Harmondsworth, Penguin Books, 1971).

Malinowski, Bronislaw, *The Family among the Australian Aborigines*, (New York, Schocken, 1913).

—*The Sexual Life of Savages in Northwestern Melanesia*, (London, Routledge and Sons, 1929).

—'Kinship', *Man* 30, 19–29, (1930).

Mauss, Marcel, 'Une catégorie de l'esprit humain: la notion de personne, celle de "moi"', [Huxley Memorial Lecture 1938], *Journal of the Royal Anthropological Institute* 68, 263–81, (1938).

—*The Gift*, translated by Ian Cunnison, [London, Routledge and Kegan Paul, 1966 (1923–24)].

Maybury-Lewis, David, 'Prescriptive Marriage Systems', *Southwestern Journal of Anthropology* 21, 207–30, (1965).

Morgan, Henry Lewis, *Systems of Consanguinity and Affinity of the Human Family*, (Washington, Smithsonian Institution, 1871).

—*Ancient Society*, (New York, Henry Holt, 1877).

Moore, Sally Falk, 'Descent and Symbolic Filiation', *American Anthropologist* 66, 1308–20, (1964).

Murdock, George, *Social Structure*, (New York, Macmillan, 1949).

—1960. 'Cognatic Forms of Social Organization', in George Murdock (ed.), *Social Structure in Southeast Asia*, New York: Wenner Gren Foundation.

Murphy, R. F., and Kasdan, L. 'The Structure of Parallel Cousin Marriage', *American Anthropologist* 61, 17–29, (1959).

Nakane, Chie, *Garos and Khasis: A Comparative Study in Matrilineal Systems*, (Paris, Mouton, 1967).

Needham, Rodney, 'A Structural Analysis of Purum Society', *American Anthropologist* 60/1, 75–101, (1958a).

—'The Formal Analysis of Prescriptive Patrilateral Cross-Cousin Marriage', *Southwestern Journal of Anthropology* 14, 199–219, (1958b).

—'Alliance and Classification among the Lamet', *Sociologus* 10/2, 97–119, (1960a).

—'Patrilateral Prescriptive Alliance and the Ungarinyin', *Southwestern Journal of Anthropology* 16, 274–91, (1960b).

—*Structure and Sentiment*, (Chicago, University of Chicago Press, 1962a).

—'Genealogy and Category in Wikmunkan Society', *Ethnology* 1, 223–64, (1962b).

—'Gurage Social and Classification: Formal Notes on an Unusual System', *Africa* 39, 153–66, (1969).

—'Remarks on the Analysis of Kinship and Marriage', in Needham (ed.), (1971).

—'Prescription', *Oceania* 42, 166–81, (1973).

—'Principles and Variations in the Structure of Sumbanese Society', in James J. Fox (ed.), *The Flow of Life*, (Cambridge, Mass. and London, Harvard University Press, 1980).

—*Mamboru: History and Structure in a Domain of Northwestern Sumba*, (Oxford, Clarendon Press, 1987).

—(ed.), *Rethinking Kinship and Marriage*, (London, Tavistock, 1971).

Östör, Ákos, Fruzzetti, Lina and Barnett, Steve, (eds), *Concepts of Person: Kinship, Caste, and Marriage in India*, (Cambridge, Mass., Havard University Press, 1982).

Overing (Kaplan), Joanna, *The Piaroa, a People of the Orinoco Basin: A Study in Kinship and Marriage*, (Oxford, Clarendon Press, 1975).

—'Dualisms as an Expression of Differences and Dangers: Marriage Exchange and Reciprocity among the Piaroa of Venezuela', in Kensinger (ed.), (1984).

Parkin, Robert, 'Ladders and Circles: Affinal Alliance and the Problem of Hierarchy'. *Man* 25/3, 472–88, (1990a).

—'Terminology and Alliance in India: Tribal Systems and the North-South Problem', *Contributions to Indian Sociology* 24/1, 61–76, (1990b).

—*The Munda of Central India: An Account of their Social Organization*, (Delhi, Oxford University Press, 1992).

—'Genealogy and Category: An Operational View', *L'Homme* 139, 85–106, (1996).

Parry, Jonathan, *Caste and Kinship in Kangra*, (London, Routledge & Kegan Paul, 1979).

HRH Prince Peter of Greece and Denmark, *A Study of Polyandry*, (The Hague, Mouton, 1963).

Radcliffe-Brown, A. R., 'The Social Organization of Australian Tribes', *Oceania* 1, 34–63, 206–46, 426–56, (1930–31).

—'Introduction', in A. R. Radcliffe-Brown and Darrell Forde (eds), *African Systems of Kinship and Marriage*, (Oxford, Oxford University Press, 1950).

—*Structure and Function in Primitive Society*, (London, Cohen and West, 1952).

Raheja, Gloria Goodwin and Gold, Ann Grodzins, *Listen to the Heron's words: Reimagining Gender and Kinship in North India*, (Berkeley, University of California Press, 1994).

Rivers, W. R. R., *The History of Melanesian Society*, 2 vols, (London, Cambridge University Press, 1914a).

—*Social Organization*, (London, Kegan Paul, Trench and Trubner, 1924).

—*Kinship and Social Organization*, [London, Athlone Press, 1968 (1914b)].

Riviere, Peter, 'Oblique Discontinuous Exchange: A New Formal Type of Prescriptive Alliance', *American Anthropologist* 68, 738–40, (1966).

—*Marriage among the Trio*, (Oxford, Clarendon Press, 1969).

—'Marriage: A Reassessment', in Rodney Needham (ed.), *Rethinking Kinship and Marriage*, (London, Tavistock, 1971).

—'Unscrambling Parenthood: The Warnock Report', *Anthropology Today* 4, 2–7, (1985).

Sahlins, Marshall, 'The Segmentary Lineage: An Organization of Predatory Expansion', *American Anthropologist* 63, 322–45, (1961).

—*Use and Abuse of Biology: An Anthropological Critique of Sociobiology*, (London, Tavistock, 1977).

Salisbury, Richard F., 'Asymmetrical Marriage Systems', *American Anthropologist* 58, 639–5, (1956).

Scheffler, Harold, 'Ancestor Worship in Anthropology: or, Observations on Descent and Descent Groups', *Current Anthropology* 7, 541–51, (1966).

—*Australian Kin Classification*, (Cambridge, Cambridge University Press, 1978).

—'Filiation and Affiliation', *Man* 20, 1–21, (1985).

—and Lounsbury, Floyd G., *A Study in Kinship Semantics: The Siriono Kinship System*, (Englewood Cliffs, Prentice-Hall, 1971).

Schneider, David, 'Some Muddles in the Models: or, How the System Really Works', in Michael Banton et al. (eds), *The Relevance of Models for Social Anthropology*, (London, Tavistock, 1962).

—'The Nature of Kinship', *Man* 64, 180–1, (1964).

—*American Kinship*, (Englewood Cliffs, Prentice-Hall, 1968).

—and Gough, Kathleen, *Matrilineal Kinship*, (Berkeley and Los Angeles, University of California Press, 1961).

Service, Elman 'Kinship Terminology and Evolution', *American Anthropologist* 62, 747–63, (1960).

*—*A Century of Controversy: Ethnological Issues from 1860 to 1960*, (Orlando, Academic Press, 1985).

*Schusky, Ernest L., *Variation in Kinship*, (New York, Holt, Rinehart and Winston, 1974).

Smith, Robert J., 'Stability in Japanese Kinship Terminology: The Historical Evidence', in Robert J. Smith and Richard K. Beardsley (eds), *Japanese Culture: Its Development and Characteristics*, (Chicago, Aldine Press, 1962).

Smith, R. T., 'The Matrifocal Family', in Jack Goody (ed.), *The Character of Kinship*, (Cambridge, Cambridge University Press 1973).

de Souseberge, L., 'Structures de parenté et d'alliance d'après les formules Pende', *Mémoires de l'Institut Royal Colonial Belge* 4, 1–93, (1955).

Spiro, Melford E., *Kinship and Marriage in Burma: A Cultural and Psychodynamic Analysis*, (Berkeley, University of California Press, 1977).

Spoehr, Alexander, 'Changing Kinship Systems: A Study in the Acculturation of the Creeks, Cherokee and Choctaw', *Field Museum of Natural History Anthropological Series* 33/4, 151–235, (1947).

Strathern, Marilyn, *The Gender of the Gift: Problems with Women and Problems with Society in Melanesia*, (Berkeley and Los Angeles, University of California Press, 1988).

—*After Nature: English Kinship in the Late Twentieth Century*, (Cambridge, Cambridge University Press, 1992).

Trautmann, Thomas, *Dravidian Kinship*, (Cambridge, Cambridge University Press, 1981).

Tyler, Stephen, 'Change in Dravidian Kinship', in J.-C. Galey (ed.), *Différences, valeurs, hiérarchie: textes offerts à Louis Dumont*, (Paris, Editions de l'EHESS, 1984).

Westermarck, Edward A., *The History of Human Marriage* (3 vols.), [London, Macmillan, 1921 (1891)].

White, Leslie A., 'What is a Classificatory Kinship Term?', *Southwestern Journal of Anthropology* 14, 378–85, (1958).

Yalman, Nur, 'The Structure of the Sinhalese Kindred: Re-examination of the Dravidian Terminology', *American Anthropologist* 64, 548–75, (1962).

Index